THE BOOK OF THE COVENANT

BY

JULIAN MORGENSTERN

HEBREW UNION COLLEGE, CINCINNATI, OHIO

Wipf & Stock
PUBLISHERS
Eugene, Oregon

Wipf and Stock Publishers
199 W 8th Ave, Suite 3
Eugene, OR 97401

The Book of the Covenant
By Morgenstern, Julian
ISBN 13: 978-1-55635-415-11
ISBN 10: 1-55635-415-0
Publication date 4/7/2007
Previously published by Hebrew Union College Annual, 1928

THE BOOK OF THE COVENANT

By JULIAN MORGENSTERN, Hebrew Union College, Cincinnati, Ohio

I

INTRODUCTION

THE basic problem in the critical study of the Book of the Covenant is altogether different from that attendant upon our investigation of the Kenite Document. Here it is the problem of the determination of the various strata of a document, which, it is manifest almost on the surface, is composite, and of the historic and religious significance of these various strata and of the composite document as a whole.

The hypotheses which have been advanced regarding the literary history of the Book of the Covenant cover a wide range indeed, though by no means as extensive as in the case of the Kenite Document. There is a practical unanimity of opinion among Biblical scholars that the Book of the Covenant is a part of the Elohist Code; but not all are clear as to whether they regard it as an integral part of this Code, or as an older piece of writing incorporated by editorial processes into E. The hypothesis most generally accepted is that developed by Baentsch,[1] that the Book of the Covenant is pre-prophetic in character, and was compiled in the Northern Kingdom towards the end of the 9th or in the early part of the 8th century B.C., and was later incorporated editorially into E. He contends, and undoubtedly correctly, that the cultural background of the laws of C is not at all that of the desert and of the age of Moses, but is rather that of the Northern Kingdom and of an age when the agricultural life and the social and religious institutions had already experienced a considerable development. Moreover, Baentsch recognizes that those laws which parallel the laws of K are, in the main

[1] *Das Bundesbuch*, 1892, and *Handkommentar zu Exodus, Leviticus und Numeri*, 1903.

at least, later than and dependent upon their K parallels. This fact, too, precludes an all too early date.

On the other hand, a judgment in extreme opposition to this is offered by Eerdmans.[2] He holds that the Book of the Covenant is a literary unit and the product of the Mosaic age. His arguments are almost entirely negative in character, i. e. he regards the evidence cited by Baentsch and others for a later date and for composition in the Northern Kingdom as invalid, or at least as of little or no significance, and maintains that the religious, social and cultural background of C could be quite as much that of the age of Moses as of a later time. He offers little or no positive evidence, however, to establish his contention that C is the actual product of the age of Moses.

Two interesting variations of the generally accepted hypothesis of Baentsch and others have been advanced. Kuenen[3] suggested, that the Book of the Covenant does not stand in its original position, that actually it represents Moses' last revelation of law to Israel just before his death, and must have stood originally where Deuteronomy stands now, and that it was removed from this, its first and logical place, and inserted in its present position by Deuteronomic writers or editors who coveted its original position for their own code. It is indeed a daring and suggestive hypothesis, and the standing of its author as a Biblical scholar, as well as certain significant statements in the early chapters of Deuteronomy, which we shall have to consider in detail in the proper place, entitle this hypothesis to at least respectful consideration. Quite interesting, although advanced haltingly and entirely as a hypothesis unsupported by direct evidence, is the suggestion of Carpenter[4] that the Book of the Covenant, with its laws of various kinds, ought to be correlated with the different laws which, according to Ex. 18. 16, Moses communicated to Israel at the Tent of Meeting. Paralleling this hypothesis

---

[2] *Alttestamentliche Studien*, III, 121–131.
[3] Cited by Carpenter and Harford, *The Composition of the Hexateuch*, 208 f. I have not been able to locate the original of this citation.
[4] *Op. cit.*, 209.

somewhat is that of Reuss,[5] that the Book of the Covenant is the product of the Southern Kingdom and of the reign of Jehosaphat. He bases his hypothesis upon a literal acceptance of the tradition recorded in II Chron. 17. 7—9 and 19. 5 ff. as historical, and an altogether gratuitous identification of the "Book of the Law of Yahwe" of 17. 9 with the Book of the Covenant. In similar manner, and with equal lack of evidence, Stade[6] maintains that the Book of the Covenant was compiled in the Southern Kingdom, but during the reign of Manasseh, and therefore preceded by but a few years the Deuteronomic Code, which is, in turn, partly dependent upon it.

Furthermore, since Baentsch's important monograph appeared,[7] Biblical scholars, with apparently the single outstanding exception of Eerdmans, have agreed that the Book of the Covenant is not a literary unit, but is composed of two disticnt strata, the one consisting of the "words" (דברים), Ex. 20. 23–26; 22. 27–30, and 23. 10–19, coupled with a brief narrative setting in 24. 3–8, and the other consisting of the remaining laws of this Book, designated by the general title "judgments" (משפטים), and contained in 21. 1—22. 26 and 23. 1–9. However, not all the laws of this latter group are actually "judgments"; rather, the original group of "judgments" has been supplemented by a considerable number of other laws, some of them of a peculiar and quite distinctive form, and in large part Deuteronomic in content and spirit and of editorial character.

In the article which immediately precedes this in this series of studies,[8] we have had occasion to discuss in detail the close relationship between the laws of the Kenite Document and their parallels in the Book of the Covenant. We have concluded that in the main the K version of these laws is the older, and in its present wording is closer to the original version of these laws than is the version in C. We have con-

---

[5] *Die Geschichte der Heiligen Schrift des Alten Testaments*, 231–234.
[6] *Geschichte des Volkes Israel*, I, 635–638.
[7] *Das Bundesbuch*, 1892.
[8] "The Oldest Document of the Hexateuch," *HUCA*, IV (1927), 1–138.

cluded, moreover, that the Kenite Document was composed in the Southern Kingdom in 899 B.C., under Kenite or Rechabite influence, and constituted the literary basis or program of the religious reformation in the fifteenth year of Asa. We have likewise concluded that the Kenite Document, or at least the laws thereof, its most essential part, were transmitted to the Northern Kingdom by Jonadab ben Rechab fifty-seven years later, were modified somewhat to adapt them to the more advanced economic and cultural conditions obtaining there at that time, and constituted the basis of the religious portion of the reformation and political revolution sponsored by Elisha, Jehu and Jonadab ben Rechab in 842 B.C. This conclusion implies, of course, that the Book of the Covenant is not a literary unit, that only those laws, the "words," unmistakable in form and content, which parallel or are manifestly of the same class as the laws of K, and also, of course, the narrative setting, are integral in this document, and that all the remaining laws are secondary and insertions into the main document. This article will endeavor to present further evidence in support of these conclusions and also to develop these conclusions further along lines of far-reaching significance for the study of Israel's history, and particularly of its religious, social and economic evolution.

As with our study of the Kenite Document, it will be well to begin our analysis of the Book of the Covenant with a detailed consideration of its narrative setting, before we undertake the analysis of its laws.

II

Exodus 24. 3–8

Scholars have long recognized that Ex. 23. 20–33 have no relation whatsoever to C, but are partly Elohistic and partly Deuteronomic. 24. 1–2 and 9–11 are unmistakably J. Moreover vv. 9–11 are obviously the direct continuation of vv. 1–2; vv. 3–8, which have no manifest connection either with what precedes or what follows, disturb this continuity.

The relation of vv. 3-8, however, to the Book of the Covenant is almost self-evident. These verses tell of a covenant entered into between Yahwe and Israel upon the basis of a body of דברים, "words," impliedly just spoken by Yahwe to Moses, and now in turn communicated by Moses to Israel. Israel, hearing these words, by formal declaration accepts them and obligates itself to keep them. Then through the performance of the proper blood-rite an everlasting, binding covenant is solemnized between the Deity and the people.

It is clear at a glance that this narrative parallels in practically every essential detail the account of the solemnization of the covenant which, we have seen, must have stood once in K, and of which a fragment is preserved in Ex. 34. 27 f.[9] This fragment there tells how, at Yahwe's bidding, Moses writes down the "words" which Yahwe had just spoken to him, and which he was, in turn, to communicate to Israel, and of which this written document was to be the permanent record. As we have seen, the remainder of the K account of the actual solemnization of the covenant has been lost, or, more likely, has been purposely suppressed by the J editors, who incorporated K into their document.

The narrative in Ex. 24. 3-8 parallels this narrative of K exactly. This is in itself cogent proof, on the one hand, that these verses belong to C, and, on the other hand, of the close relationship existing between K and C, at least in the latter's original form.

Careful examination of these verses reveals one disturbing element, viz. v. 3. This verse tells that Moses came and recited to the people all the "words" of Yahwe and all the "judgments," and the people, hearing these, answered promptly and unanimously, "All the 'words' which Yahwe hath spoken, we will do." It is clear that the several statements of this verse are out of place here; they come too soon in the narrative, and, moreover, are repeated later, and with greater exactness in their proper place in the narrative. Thus, for example, the first statement, that Moses came to the people, manifestly from the place of Yahwe's revelation of the laws

[9] Cf. "The Oldest Document of the Hexateuch," *HUCA*, IV (1927), 95 ff.

to him, comes too soon. For v. 4 tells that Moses wrote down all the "words" of Yahwe, and this was impliedly at Yahwe's bidding and in His presence, just as the parallel narrative in Ex. 34. 27 f. tells. Furthermore, v. 7 tells in the proper place in the narrative, that after having made all necessary preparations for the formal solemnization of the covenant, Moses read the laws to the people from the book or scroll in which he had inscribed them. And there, too, and likewise in its proper place in the narrative, we are told that the people formally accepted the covenant with the words, "All that Yahwe hath spoken we will do and we will obey." Clearly v. 7 b is the original of that which is anticipated and repeated unduly and in improper place in v. 3 b.

One further and very significant discrepancy exists between v. 3 and the remainder of the narrative. V. 3 tells that Moses recites to the people not only the "words" of Yahwe but also the "judgments." It is self-evident that משפטים is used here in a technical sense, and refers to that particular group of laws beginning in 21. 2, and designated specifically in 21. 1 by this term. This is further and very convincing evidence that 24. 3–8 must be correlated with the laws of C, and not with any other body of laws, as, for example, the Ten Commandments in 20. 2–17, as has been not infrequently maintained. But it is significant that outside of this one passage, the remainder of the narrative makes reference only to the "words," and is completely silent with regard to the "judgments," even in places where there was quite as much reason to mention the "judgments" along with the "words" as in v. 3 a. Thus v. 4 states explicitly that Moses wrote down the "words," but is silent as to the "judgments," and v. 7 a implies that it is the written record of the "words," which constitutes the "Book of the Covenant." And even more significant, v. 8 says explicitly that Yahwe makes the covenant with Israel upon the basis of "all these 'words,'" and makes no mention of the "judgments" whatsoever.[10]

---

[10] Significantly enough, even v. 3 b mentions only the "words" as the actual basis of the covenant, and, despite the specific reference thereto in 3 a, is entirely silent as to the "judgments."

But one conclusion can be drawn from all this evidence, viz. that v. 3 is not original here, but is editorial, and was inserted here for some specific purpose, which seemingly has to do with that particular group of laws designated technically as the "judgments." What this purpose may have been we shall determine later. Moreover, it is clear that with v. 3 omitted, vv. 4–8 offer a narrative complete in all essential details, and with unity more pronounced than with v. 3 retained.

In vv. 4–8 it is possible, and in fact quite probable, that v. 4 b, telling of the erection of the twelve stone pillars to correspond to the twelve tribes of Israel, is a gloss. Not that it is out of harmony with the rest of the narrative or with the religious principles and institutions obtaining at the time of the composition of the Book of the Covenant, but solely because these twelve stone pillars play no rôle at all in the narrative. Originally, as we know from abundant evidence, sacred stone pillars served in early Semitic religion as the abodes of local deities or spirits or else, in later stages of religious evolution, as the symbols of deities. These deities were, of course, largely, if not entirely non-Yahwistic in character. But in this portion of the C narrative the altar alone is the symbol of Yahwe. Upon it the sacrifices are offered as a matter of course, and likewise upon it Moses pours one half of the blood of the covenant, while the other half is sprinkled upon the people. And since Yahwe and the people are the two contracting parties in this covenant, upon whom, according to the implied customary ritual of blood covenant, the blood of the covenant-sacrifice was poured, and since one half of the blood was sprinkled upon the people and the other half upon the altar, it follows that the altar here, and it alone, was regarded as the concrete symbol of Yahwe. Manifestly, therefore, there is no essential rôle in the narrative for the twelve pillars. Moreover, since the covenant is explicitly established with all Israel as one people, there is not the slightest reason or excuse for representing the people in any way as a federation of twelve tribes, twelve subordinate units. These considerations make it extremely probable that v. 4 b is not a part of the original C narrative.

But unquestionably this gloss was inserted here at a comparatively early date. For it is inconceivable that such a reference to twelve sacred stone pillars set up alongside of an altar of Yahwe, and in connection with the solemnization of a religious ceremony of such basic significance in the religion of Israel, should have been made later than Deuteronomy.[11] The gloss is unquestionably pre-Deuteronomic, and must therefore be assigned in all likelihood to those Elohist editors who, as we shall see, incorporated the Book of the Covenant into their document. This conclusion suggests a ready and simple explanation of this insertion. The classic Elohist account of the solemnization of a covenant between Yahwe and Israel is found in Josh. 24. There there is no mention of altar, sacrifice or sprinkling of covenant-blood. But there, as here, Joshua writes down the words or terms of the covenant in the "Book of the Law of God"[12] and then sets up a great stone. That this was a sacred stone may be inferred from the fact, recorded in v. 26, that it stood in the sanctuary[13] of Yahwe. This stone is represented by the Elohist authors of this passage as the eternal sign or witness of the covenant just entered into by Yahwe and Israel. Quite similarly these same Elohist writers tell that the twelve stones, which, at Joshua's command, the people take up from the temporarily dry bed of the Jordan, and set up at Gilgal on the western bank of the river, were to symbolize the twelve tribes of Israel, and to serve as a constant sign of the miracle wrought by Yahwe in their behalf.[14]

Undoubtedly the Elohist editors of the Book of the Covenant must have missed in this account of the solemnization of the covenant one element which to them seemed all important, the sacred stone pillar or pillars, which were to be unto Israel the eternal witnesses of their covenant with

---

[11] Cf. Deut. 16. 22.

[12] It is rather surprising that Reuss did not correlate this "Book of the Law of God," instead of the Book of the Covenant, with the "Book of the Law of Yahwe" of II Chron. 17. 9.

[13] במקוש, literally, "in the sacred precincts"; cf. the Arabic ḥimā, and Robertson Smith, *The Religion of the Semites*[2], index under ḥimā.

[14] Josh. 4. 3, 9, 20.

Yahwe. Accordingly they inserted a reference to such pillars at what seemed to them the logical place, and just as in connection with the Gilgal episode, so here too they made these pillars twelve in number to conform to the twelve tribes of Israel. Recognizing Ex. 24.4b as the work of RE, and therefore omitting it from the main narrative, we find that this narrative now reads with perfect completeness and smoothness.[15]

A few facts in this narrative of interest and of some significance for this study may be pointed out. Moses is here the chief, or rather, the sole functionary. Yahwe has already communicated the "words" to him; he now writes them down, and then reads them to the people from his written record. He is therefore the intermediary between Yahwe and Israel. There are no priests as yet, nor is the offering of sacrifices as yet the function of priests. Instead the youths of Israel offer the sacrifices, but Moses alone functions in the covenant-ceremony proper. The sacrifice consists of bullocks, certainly not the standard sacrifice of a people dwelling, even though temporarily, in the desert. Cows and bullocks are rather uncommon domestic animals in the desert, owing to their need of comparatively frequent watering. Camels, sheep and goats are instead the regular domestic animals of the desert, and those regularly offered as sacrifice. On the other hand, bullocks, because of their size and correspondingly large value, represent the highest type of sacrifice among Semitic agricultural peoples. In the Biblical ritual they play just this rôle. Manifestly, therefore, the point of view in these verses is that of the settled, agricultural life of Palestine, rather than that of the desert and of the age of Moses.

It is not without significance too that Moses first sprinkles half of the blood upon the altar, then reads the "words" to the people and hears their formal acceptance of the covenant,

---

[15] Perhaps, too, these twelve pillars, corresponding to the traditional twelve tribes, serve an additional purpose, to represent, in accordance with basic prophetic doctrine, that Yahwe was the God of all Israel, and not merely of either the Northern or the Southern Kingdom alone, and that His covenant was with entire Israel, and not only with a part thereof.

and only then sprinkles the other half of the blood upon
them. One might at first expect that the blood would be
sprinkled upon both altar and people at the same time.
But a moment's thought makes the reason for the procedure here
clear. As we have seen, the altar here is the concrete and
visible symbol of Yahwe. It is Yahwe who has, impliedly
at least, proposed, and who therefore need make no further
declaration of His readiness to enter into the covenant.
Accordingly, the covenant-blood can be sprinkled upon the
altar immediately, and the people understand the full implication of this rite. But the "words," which as yet the
people have not heard, must first be read to them by Moses,
and must be formally accepted by them before the covenant-
blood can be sprinkled upon them. But even before the
people have actually heard the "words," they have been
made to realize, by the sprinkling of the blood upon the
altar, that Yahwe, on His part, is ready to enter into covenant
with them, and that the matter therefore awaits only their
affirmation.

Manifestly, too, the narrative is not altogether complete. Its conclusion has been lost; but this we can easily
supply. For unquestionably, in accordance with the principles of early Semitic religious practice, the animals here
sacrificed not only provided the blood for the covenant-
ceremony, but likewise constituted a covenant-sacrifice, par-
ticipated in by the people as the guests of the Deity. In fact
just this is implied in the designation of these sacrifices in
v. 5 as $z^ebahim\ šelamim$. This sacrificial meal constituted an
additional rite of solemnization of the covenant between
Yahwe and Israel, supplementing the sprinkling of the blood.

Finally, it should be noted that the "words" are here
inscribed, not upon stone tablets, but upon a scroll. This
is in significant contrast to the parallel statement, in Ex. 34.
27 f., that at Yahwe's command Moses inscribed the "words"
of the covenant, according to K, upon two tablets. But, as
we have suggested,[16] it is quite probable that the reference

[16] "The Oldest Document, &c.," *HUCA*, IV (1927), 97.

to the two stone tablets there is editorial; and in such case it would be equally probable that the original K narrative told, or at least understood, that, just as here, the "words" there were likewise written by Moses upon a scroll.

The obvious relation to and dependence upon the Kenite Document of the Book of the Covenant raise the important question whether the latter did not have originally a larger narrative setting than merely Ex. 24. 4–8. We have seen that the original Kenite code of laws was embedded in a narrative setting of considerable extent, which must have told of the early life of Moses, his flight from Egypt and marriage into the Kenite tribe; of his first contact with Yahwe and the charge laid upon him to go back to Egypt and bring his brethren out from there to the sacred mountain in the desert where Yahwe was dwelling; of Moses' fulfillment of this charge, of Yahwe's command to him to lead the people away from there, of the revelation of the divine name and of the "words," of the solemnization of the covenant upon the basis of these "words," of the erection of the "tent of meeting" and the institution of revelation by means of the oracle; of the visit of Moses' brother-in-law and the appointment of the judges at his suggestion, of Moses' plea to his brother-in-law to be Israel's guide through the desert and of Hobab's finally yielding to this plea; of the brief journey of the people through the desert and their approach to, conquest of and settlement in the extreme southern part of Palestine. Without this narrative the K account of the covenant between Yahwe and Israel would have been incomplete and not altogether comprehensible.

Now it is quite probable that the Book of the Covenant may have contained originally a similar, and even parallel narrative introduction and conclusion. For here too the account of the solemnization alone is quite as incomplete and incomprehensible without the appropriate narrative setting, recounting the events leading up to the solemnization of the covenant, and the incidents following upon this, whereby Yahwe fulfilled His part of the covenant. The very abruptness with which the "words" in Ex. 20. 23 begin, and the fact that, as we have seen,[17] the first "word" has been suppressed in favor of the editorial v. 22, and the additional fact that, again as we have seen,[18] the revelation of a code of "words" designed to be the basis of a covenant between a deity and a people which had, impliedly, not known nor worshiped him before, necessitated a statement, brief though it may have been, of the actual name of the deity, in order that the people might thereafter worship him specifically by name, make it quite certain that the Book of the Covenant must have possessed originally a narrative setting of some extent, even though this may not have equalled in range of content the original narrative setting of the Kenite Document. Unfortunately, however, the entire narrative introduction of C has apparently been suppressed by the Elohist editors in favor of their own narrative.[19]

[17] *Ibid.*, 71.
[18] *Ibid.*, 31 f.
[19] It is, of course, not impossible, nor even improbable, that some small fragments of the original narrative introduction of the Book of the Covenant may be preserved in the early chapters of Exodus, just as, as we have seen (*ibid.*, 51–54, 119–135), was the case with K. We would expect to find such fragments of the C narrative in passages ordinarily assigned to E. It is by no means impossible that the nucleus of Ex. 3. 1–15 (cf. my "The Elohist Narrative in Exodus 3. 1–15," *AJSL*, XXXVII [1921], 242–262), may come from C, although, if so, it has probably been considerably reworked by Elohist editors. There is nothing in the present text to forbid this hypothesis, although, it must be admitted, there is likewise little direct evidence in support of it. Indirectly, however, a number of significant details in that narrative favor this hypothesis. Certainly the conception of Yahwe dwelling in the סנה upon the sacred mountain, is very old, and parallels appropriately the K conception of Yahwe dwelling upon the sacred mountain with the cave of revelation thereon. This ancient, local conception of Deity would be more natural and appropriate in the older Book of the Covenant than in the younger Elohist Code. Furthermore, the representation of the Deity of this mountain as the God of Moses' חתן, as we have had to emend the אביך of v. 6 and the אבתיכם of v. 15, conforms exactly to the conception of the Deity which we have found characteristic of K. The same conclusion holds true of the designation here of the people merely as the בני ישראל, and not yet as Yahwe's people; for, as we have seen, this was likewise the procedure in K, and not until the covenant had been solemnized, could Israel be rightfully designated as "Yahwe's people." Moreover, understanding that the C narrative, like that of K, was anticipating the coming of Israel, after its deliverance from Egypt, to the sacred mountain in the desert and the establish-

THE BOOK OF THE COVENANT

Unquestionably the Book of the Covenant must have contained originally an account of Israel's coming to the sacred place and of the events leading immediately to the revelation of the "words" and the solemnization of the covenant. For in the light of the manifest parallelism of C with K, it is impossible to conceive that C could have told of the revelation of the "words" and the solemnization of the covenant without some appropriate motivation. But what that may have been, and whether it paralleled in any way the account which must once have stood in K, viz. the original form of the golden calf story,[20]. it is impossible to tell, although this is by no means impossible or improbable.

We have seen, too, that the K narrative told of Israel's journey from the sacred mountain of Yahwe under the leadership of Moses and with the guidance of Moses' brother-in-law, Hobab, until they entered, conquered and settled down in southern Palestine. Presumably therefore the C narrative must have contained some parallel *motif* of divinely appointed guidance of Israel through the desert. And here expectation is not disappointed. The Pentateuch records five different, contradictory and mutually exclusive accounts of

ing of the covenant there between it and Yahwe, the statement of v. 12b becomes much more intelligible, viz. that when Moses should have brought the people out from Egypt they would worship Yahwe at this mountain. Nor is it entirely out of possible accord with the narrative introduction of C that Yahwe should have revealed His real name to Moses at this, His first contact with him, rather than later, as in K, just before the actual solemnization of the covenant.

This evidence is, of course, too indirect and insufficient to posit absolutely that the nucleus of the narrative of Ex. 3. 1–15 was drawn from C, but it does suffice to make the hypothesis attractive.

Not improbably, too, certain elements of the plague narrative may have been drawn from the original introduction to C, but if so, it is hardly possible to identify them, for they would seem to be rather elements of the narrative itself, than of the present literary form thereof. Nor is it possible to assign any portion of Ex. 19 or 20. 1–21 to C. We must therefore conclude that by far the greater part, if not actually all of the original introduction of C has been suppressed by the Elohist editors in favor of their own narrative, or if not this, then that it has been lost in some other way. But that there was originally a narrative introduction to C similar to that of K, though not necessarily of the same extent, we need not hesitate to believe.

[20] Cf. "The Oldest Document, &c.," *HUCA*, IV (1927), 106 ff.

the way in which Israel was guided through the desert.[21] Four of these five accounts have been assigned to specific sources on the ground of abundant and convincing evidence. The account of the guidance by Hobab has been assigned to K, that by the pillar of cloud by day and the pillar of fire by night to J, that by the angel or messenger of Yahwe to E, and that by the k*e*bod Yahwe to P. But one account remains unassigned, as yet, viz. the account in Num. 10. 33 b.

III

NUMBERS 10. 33b

This half-verse says that "the ark of the covenant of Yahwe was journeying on a three days stretch in advance of Israel in order to spy out a resting-place for them." The half-verse is appended to the K account of the selection of Hobab as Israel's guide. Manifestly it not only has nothing to do with this narrative, but is absolutely contradictory to it. If Israel was guided by Hobab, there was no need nor possibility of its being guided by the ark; and *vice versa*, if it was guided by the ark, there was no need nor possibility of Hobab's guidance. Manifestly the two accounts must come from different sources. And this consideration suggests too that this little narrative of Israel's guidance by the ark must come from some source entirely independent of not only K, but also of J, E and P. What source can this be? Either we must posit some source, or at least some tradition, entirely independent of K, J, E or P, and also of C, or we must attempt to correlate this fragmentary narrative with C.[22] Certainly the latter seems the more reasonable procedure; and, as we shall see, it has much evidence in its favor.

---

[21] Cf. my "Biblical Theophanies," *ZA*, XXV (1912), 139–193 and XXVIII (1915), 15–60; also my "The Oldest Document, &c.," *HUCA*, IV (1927), 41 f.

[22] It is, of course, needless to discuss the possibility of assigning this narrative to D, the only remaining document of the Hexateuch, since, as is generally recognized, D has no independent account of the Exodus and the wilderness wanderings, but is dependent entirely upon the traditions of the older sources, particularly E.

In its present connection v. 33 b seems to be harmonized with the K account of Hobab's guidance, immediately preceding, by the insertion of the words, דרך שלשת ימים. These words seem to imply in this connection that Hobab was Israel's actual and immediate guide, ever present with it and pointing out the way it must go, while the ark kept a three days journey in advance of the host of Israel, in order to search out for it a resting-place, presumably in this connection the nightly camping-place. For if the actual guide of Israel was Hobab, then it must have been he and no other person or agency, such as the ark, who determined and brought Israel to its final goal. Therefore in this connection מנוחה could not designate the final goal of its journeying, and could accordingly mean only the nightly camping-place.[23]

But a moment's thought shows the incongruity of this idea. What sense could there be in having the ark journey on three days in advance of the host of Israel, even for the purpose of fixing the nightly camping-places? It was one of the necessary functions of the guide to determine before the beginning of the day's march, just where the people would encamp at night. Moreover, with the ark constantly three

[23] Just this is the reinterpretation of this passage which Deut. 1. 33 gives, when it says that Yahwe was going before Israel along the way through the desert in order to spy out for it a place where it might encamp. For unquestionably the use of the word לתור here, as well as the general connection, indicate a dependence of this passage upon Num. 10. 33 b. Manifestly the Deuteronomist did not read דרך שלשת ימים in his version of Num. 10. 33 b, for otherwise he could not have told that Yahwe journeyed on immediately ahead of Israel to spy out its nightly camping-place. Manifestly too, he deliberately suppressed all reference to the ark, and substituted for it Yahwe Himself. His reason for this we shall learn later.

Quite obviously the association of the ark with Israel's מנוחה, the goal of its journeying through the desert and the land of its permanent sojourn, with Yahwe dwelling in its midst in the Temple, is reflected in Ps. 132. 8, קומה יהוה למנוחתך אתה וארון עזך, and in I Chron. 28. 2, where the Temple is called בית מנוחה לארון. In both these passages, and also in Ps. 132. 14, מנחה means a permanent dwelling-place, and not a place of temporary sojourn, such as a nightly camping-place would be. Unquestionably these three passages, so obviously dependent upon Num. 10. 33 b, likewise did not read דרך שלשת ימים there, and accordingly interpreted מנוחה in this verse, just as we have done, as the permanent goal of Israel's journey through the desert, the land promised to it by Yahwe.

days in advance of Israel, how could its connection and means of communication with Israel be maintained? And finally, if the entire journey from the Mountain of Yahwe to the goal of Israel's journeying in southern Palestine, according to the K narrative, was one of but three days, then certainly there was no place for the ark three days in advance of Israel's host; for it would have been at the very goal of the journey even before Israel had set out, and there would have been no need for it to travel on further, as the term לָנוּעַ implies. Quite certainly the words דרך שלשת ימים have no place here, and are a very disturbing insertion into the original text.[24] Either they are the unintentional result of dittography resulting from the rereading of the same words in the first half of the verse, or they are a harmonistic insertion, designed to soften somewhat the otherwise absolute contradiction existing between v. 33 b and the narrative of Hobab's guidance immediately preceding it.

For with these words omitted this contradiction becomes much more absolute and glaring. The half-verse now states explicitly that the ark of the covenant of Yahwe was journeying on before Israel in order to search out for it a resting-place, i. e. the final goal of its journeying. How long this journeying and this manner of guidance endured, is not stated nor implied in any way. Nor is there the slightest implication of where this goal lay, whether in southern Palestine or farther to the north or east, or whether the approach of Israel to its final home in Palestine was through the south, as in the K narrative, or through the country to the east of the Jordan. Only one thing this verse does imply, and this very positively, that Israel journeyed on steadily under the guidance of the ark until it reached the final goal of its journeying. This tradition knows absolutely nothing of an interrupted journey and of a forty years sojourn and wandering in the desert, but only of a direct, unbroken journey from the place of revelation and solemnization of the covenant to the final destination, the land which, this half-verse implies, Yahwe must have promised to them. In other words, this

[24] So practically all modern commentators.

half-verse too tells, or at least implies, that Yahwe immediately and without the slightest delay fulfilled His part of His covenant with Israel. In this it agrees completely with the K narrative, and disagrees with the younger J and E narrative of the forty years of wandering in the wilderness.

Here a question of extreme significance for this study must be answered: how was it possible for an object such as the ark actually was, to guide the people by determining the road which they must follow through the trackless desert, until they reached their goal? To this question v. 33 b gives no answer whatsoever other than to imply that this was, of course, divine guidance, that in other words, there was some direct relationship between Yahwe and the ark and between this guidance by the ark and the fulfillment of Yahwe's covenant-obligation to Israel. More than this, however, this little half-verse does not tell.

Fortunately, however, one passage in the Bible sheds abundant light upon this question. It is the narrative in I Sam. 4–6 of the capture of the ark by the Philistines and of its experiences while in their possession, or rather of their experiences with it. A number of calamities which befell them just while the ark was among them raised the suspicion in the minds of the Philistines that, even though they had captured the ark, it was by no means as impotent as they had inferred, but was still a powerful deity, or in some way associated with a powerful deity, who could work his hostile will upon them even while in their midst in their very land. The continued presence of such a powerful and hostile deity among them was dangerous, and might, if too long protracted, threaten even their complete annihilation. It behooved them to rid themselves of the ark as speedily as possible, provided, of course, that it was really the powerful and hostile god that they suspected. But of this they were not altogether certain. After all, misfortunes similar to these had befallen them before, although seemingly not simultaneously, and not under just such conditions. It might be chance and no more, and the ark therefore might have no connection whatsoever with these calamities and their coincidence. In such case it would be folly to lose for no reason whatever a trophy of victory so precious as the ark of Israel. Accordingly the Philistines resolved very naturally to put the ark to a test to determine whether it was in truth a deity, as they suspected, and, of course, the one who had brought these calamities upon them, or whether it was a mere inanimate and therefore powerless object, which could in no wise be responsible for their misfortune.

What was the test? They put the ark in a new wagon, drawn by cows which had never before been yoked. For if the ark was truly a powerful deity, it must be treated with all honor. For this same reason they gave it proper tribute, which they put in the wagon alongside of the ark. Thereupon they let the wagon, with the ark upon it and the cows pulling it, go and watched carefully to see which road it would take; for the test which they proposed was this, if the ark would take the road leading up to Beth Shemesh, i. e. back into the land of Israel, they would know that it was truly a god, indeed a powerful deity, who had brought all these calamities upon them, and of whom therefore they would be well rid. But if it did not take this road, but remained, no matter by what other road the cows might go, in the land of the Philistines, they would know that it was no deity at all, but only an inanimate object, which had no relation whatever to their misfortunes; and since it would still be in their own land, it would be easy for them to regain, or rather to keep possession of it. This was the test.

Now on the surface this test seems to have been just a mere matter of chance which road the cows would take. There were two or more roads leading away from Ekron, or whichever Philistine city was the last abiding-place of the ark, one of which led up to Beth Shemesh, and the other or others led in various directions through the Philistine country. The chances therefore were even, or two to one, or perhaps more, according to the number of roads leading through Philistia, that the cows would remain in Philistine country and the ark be pronounced an irresponsible, inanimate object. Such seems on the surface to have been the character of the test.

But just this was what the test was not. It was not a matter of chance at all. It should be noted first that these cows had never been yoked before, i.e. had never been trained to pull a wagon. Ordinarily, therefore, in this their first experience under the yoke, they would in all likelihood not pull together, but rather pulling unevenly and ofttimes against each other, the wagon would not move or would be pulled hither and thither without getting anywhere, certainly not as far as Beth Shemesh. In the second place, as v. 7 states explicitly, they were cows which had recently given birth and were now suckling their calves. The calves were shut up at home, so that they could not follow their mothers. The natural instinct of the cows, therefore, would have been to turn right around and go back to their calves. Manifestly the Philistines designedly made it as difficult as possible for the ark to reach Beth Shemesh. But, as v. 12 states in significant detail, the cows took the straight road along the highway to Beth Shemesh, lowing as they went along, but turning neither to the right nor to the left, until they came to the Israelite village. Now the lowing of the cows, mentioned explicitly, is significant. They were, of course, lowing for their young, presumably in answer to the lowing of the latter to them. It implies that their strong instinct was to turn around and go back to their calves, and that they would have done this, had they been able. But some power or force made this impossible for them, and drove them unerringly and irresistibly along the road which it had chosen. And it reached its appointed goal despite all these obstacles which the Philistines had purposely put in its way. This irresistible power or force was the ark, or emanated from the ark. The test proposed and executed by the Philistines therefore was the ability of the ark to select for itself a specified road leading to a fixed goal, and, in the face of their inexperience and natural unwillingness, to drive the cows pulling the wagon upon which it rested along this road of its own choosing until it should reach its goal. And seeing the final outcome of the test, which they had themselves proposed, the Philistines were satisfied that this ark was indeed the cause of all their misfortunes, and were happy to be thus rid of this powerful and dangerous deity.

Here then is a specific case, recorded in the Bible, and unquestionably of great antiquity, of the ark selecting the road it wanted to go, and driving its bearers, or whatever means of locomotion may have been employed, irresistibly along this road.[25]

Now exactly some such procedure as this is implied in Num. 10. 33 b. However, since cows or oxen are domestic animals comparatively rare in the desert, and since likewise transportation by means of wagons is rendered difficult, if not practically impossible, by the character of the desert terrain, we must picture the ark as carried along upon the shoulders of bearers properly qualified for that task. But it was not these bearers nor their leader who determined the direction which the ark should take, but it was the ark itself, or the power resident within the ark, which discharged this function.[26] These facts, and, as we shall establish, the

[25] Interesting reminiscences of this tradition are preserved in the Midrash and show that the Rabbis of old had a strong feeling for the original meaning of the narrative of I Sam. 6. *Bammidbar Rabba* XXI, 12 tells that when the Philistines were about to put the ark in the wagon, it raised itself up and set itself upon the wagon. And IV, 19 tells that the ark was able of old to carry its carriers as well as itself, that, in other words, it could drive its carriers along the road which it wished to go.

[26] This concept is by no means uncommon in Semitic religious practice and folk-lore. According to Macrobius (*Saturnalia*, I, 23, 10) " the Syrians used to worship the sun, under the name of Jove, whom they called Δία Ἡλιου-πολίτην, with most elaborate ceremonies in the city known as Heliopolis... For an image of the Heliopolitan god was carried about in a litter, just as the images of the gods are borne in the celebration of the Circensian games, and many nobles of the province, with shaven heads and having practiced chastity for a long time, would carry it, and would be borne along by the divine spirit, not by their own volition but just as if the god was driving his bearers."

In quite the same manner, according to Lucian (*De Dea Syra*, 36 f. [ed. Jacobitz, 358]) the image of Apollo at Hierapolis would drive its priestly bearers backward and forward, hither and thither, and by the direction in which it would drive them it would foretell future events. It would likewise at times lift itself from off their shoulders and rise into the air and remain suspended there for some time entirely of its own accord.

In modern Semitic folk-practice similar powers are frequently ascribed to the corpses of saints or other holy persons, especially while being borne to their

manifestly important rôle which the ark played in the narrative of the Book of the Covenant, compel us to consider the history of the ark in full detail.

last resting-places. Thus Klunzinger relates (*Upper Egypt, Its People and Products*, 393), " The body of such saints, when on its way to its last resting-place, has such a mysterious power on those that carry the bier that they can do nothing of themselves, but are compelled to follow a certain route, and bury the saint in whatever spot he may choose. An old negro slave in Kosseir, well-known for his long, harmless, pious life, having died towards evening, would not, on any account, have himself buried the same evening, and the bearers, in spite of all their shouting of *la ilah ill Allah*, could not bring the corpse to the graveyard. It remained, therefore, all night in the house (though the people do not like to keep a corpse a night), watched by a multitude of people praying. Next morning also it could not be buried for a long time; the blessed dead compelled the bearers to go through all the streets of the town, till at last, on the recommendation of the more enlightened governor, the higher officials carried the bier to the grave; even the Turkish soldiers could not accomplish it. The whole town was in uproar. The Mohammedans say the angels exercise this coercive power, the Christians believe it is the devil. Deceit or practical joking is not always to be surmised in such cases; on the occasion just mentioned almost the whole male population tried what they could do, and among them many staid and serious men. It is the firm belief of these people that the deceased saint or the angels cause the pressure, and then they feel it too. Even in Cairo such occurrences are common as well as in the other parts of the country. Among the ancient Egyptians also the processions of the images of their deities did not direct themselves at pleasure, but by divine inspiration."

Another instance of this same belief and practice, recorded by Lane (*An Account of the Manners and Customs of the Modern Egyptians*, 479 [edition of 1890]) illustrates well the supposed power of the corpse to resist being carried elsewhere than whither it wishes to go, as well as the manifestly modern belief that it is possible to deceive the corpse, if this be advisable. " Very often, it is said, a welee impels the bearers of his corpse to a particular spot... The following anecdote, describing an ingenious mode of puzzling a dead saint in a case of this kind, was related to me by one of my friends... Some men were lately bearing the corpse of a welee to a tomb prepared for it in the great cemetery on the north of the metropolis; but, on arriving at the gate called Báb en-Nasr, which leads to this cemetery, they found themselves unable to proceed farther from the cause above mentioned. 'It seems,' said one of the bearers, ' that the sheykh is determined not to be buried in the cemetery of Báb en-Nasr: and what shall we do?' They were all much perplexed: but being as obstinate as the saint himself, they did not immediately yield to his caprice. Retreating a few paces, and then advancing with a quick step, they thought, by such an impetus, to force the corpse through the gateway; but their efforts were unsuccessful; and the same experiment they repeated in vain several times. They then placed the bier on the ground to rest and consult; and one of them, beckoning away his comrades to a distance beyond the hearing of the dead saint, said to them, 'Let us take up

IV

THE ARK OF YAHWE

In recent years this subject has been repeatedly investigated by eminent Biblical scholars, and the conclusions reached by them have been presented in a number of notable monographs.[27] In general each monograph demonstrates satisfactorily the shortcomings and inadequacies of all previously presented hypotheses with regard to the origin, history and

the bier again, and turn it round quickly several times till the sheykh becomes giddy; he then will not know in what direction we are going, and we may take him easily through the gate.' This they did; the saint was puzzled as they expected; and quietly buried in the place which he had so striven to avoid."

Commenting upon a similar instance in modern Palestinian folk-lore, Canaan ("Mohammedan Saints and Sanctuaries in Palestine," *JPOS*, VII [1927], 24, note 5) says, "In many cases the first miracle performed by a *welî* after his death is in the way his body behaves while carried for burial. It may get so heavy that those carrying the coffin (*suḫliyeh*) have to stop and put down their load. On other occasions it becomes very light or even ... may fly from their shoulders." (Cf. also Canaan, "Mohammedan Saints and Sanctuaries in Palestine," *JPOS*, IV [1924], 52.) This is precisely the same procedure as that of the afore-mentioned statue of Apollo at Hierapolis.

An especially interesting and significant instance of this particular superstition is cited by Certeux and Carnoy (*L'Algérie Traditionnelle*, 110); "Before dying Sidi Mohammed ben Alya had indicated his tomb, at the spot called Ṛerizem-el-Hotob. But the camel, which carried his corpse in a kind of palanquin, ambled in the direction of Temad, without either cries or blows being able to turn it from its course. Piously, therefore, a new decision of the marabout was assumed, and he was buried at Temad."

Other instances of this superstition are cited by Kelly (*Syria and the Holy Land*, 20) and Jaussen (*Coutumes des Arabes au pays de Moab*, 105). That it was not merely corpses that were thought to possess this power, but that it might be inherent in any holy object, may be inferred from a tradition recorded by Dapper (*Asia*, I, 30b, edition of 1681) that on one occasion at Damascus oxen were unable to move a wagon containing holy earth, impliedly because it was contrary to the will of the saint or holy power associated with that earth. (Cf. also Snouck-Hurgronje, *Mekka*, II, 65.)

[27] The most important of these monographs which have appeared during the present century are Dibelius, *Die Lade Jahves* (1906); Gunkel, "Die Lade Jahves ein Thronsitz," *ZMR*, 1906; Sevensma, *De Ark Gods*, 1908 (not accessible to me); Arnold, *Ephod and Ark* (1917); Hartmann, "Zelt und Lade," *ZAW*, XXXVII (1917-1918), 209-245; Gressmann, *Die Lade Jahves*, 1920; Budde, "Ephod und Lade," *ZAW*, XXXIX (1922), 1-42; Torczyner, "Die Bundeslade und die Anfänge der Religion Israels," in *Festschrift zum 50jährigen Bestehen der Hochschule für die Wissenschaft des Judentums*, 219-297.

character of the ark and its contents and related objects, and then proceeds to advance a more or less new hypothesis, the weaknesses of which in turn are exposed with equally cogent arguments by the monograph next appearing. All these monographs deal, as a matter of course, with practically the same˙Biblical evidence, although quite naturally they stress the importance of different points, and thus arrive at their divergent conclusions. Each hypothesis, it is generally admitted, has some measure of truth; and yet not one has been found altogether convincing and acceptable. This is apparently due to one fundamental fallacy underlying the argument and conclusions of most, if not all of these scholars. It is that almost unconsciously they take it for granted that the ark was exactly the same thing, or was conceived of in exactly the same manner, throughout its entire history, at the end thereof as at the beginning, and that therefore the conclusions to be drawn with regard to it from the picture of the ark, with its two cherubim and other equipment, in the Priestly Code and other late, post-exilic writings, have quite the same significance for the history of the ark and its origins as has the evidence of the earliest records of the ark in Biblical literature. Particularly Dibelius, Gressmann and Torczyner have been led far astray by their failure to guard themselves sufficiently against this fallacy.

One fact of far-reaching significance must be kept carefully in mind here, viz. that in all likelihood the ark had disappeared by the time of the Babylonian Exile, and was therefore not present in the second Temple. This is to be inferred from the fact that in his detailed plan for the rebuilt Temple Ezekiel makes no provision whatsoever for the ark or for a place for it.[28] Even more significant is the explicit statement of Jer. 3. 16, generally recognized by Biblical scholars as a passage of post-exilic composition inserted into its present position, "It shall be when ye shall have multiplied and become fruitful in the land, that in those days—it is the

---

[28] So far as I can determine, Volz (*Die biblischen Altertümer*, 11 f.) was the first to call attention to the significance of Ezekiel's lack of provision for the ark in his plan of the rebuilt Temple.

oracle of Yahwe—the people shall say no more, 'the ark of the covenant of Yahweh,' nor shall it come into their thought, nor shall they remember it, nor shall they miss it, nor shall they make another."[29] Such an utterance would be altogether impossible were the ark, or even an ark, a substitute for the original ark, extant in the Temple. Furthermore I Mac. 1. 21-23 tells that when Antiochus invaded Jerusalem he carried away from the Temple "the golden altar, and the candlestick for the light and all its accessories, and the table of the shewbread, and the cups, and the bowls, and the golden censers, and the veil, and the crowns, and the golden adornment on the façade of the Temple, and he scaled it off. Moreover, he took the silver, and the gold, and the choice vessels; he took also the hidden treasures which he found."[29a] Manifestly Antiochus carried off every object of value upon which he could lay his hand, penetrating for this purpose as far as the very holy of holies. He even carried off the veil which separated this from the body of the Temple. Golden objects seem to have excited his cupidity especially. It is therefore extremely significant that in this long list of the holiest utensils in the Temple cult, the ark, which, according to the tradition of the Priestly Code, was covered with the golden *kapporet*, is not mentioned, particularly since, with the removal of the veil, it would have been exposed to view. There can be only one conclusion from this, viz. that Antiochus found no ark in the Temple. Significantly too, despite the explicit legislation for the ark in the Pentateuch, the Rabbis of old were apparently aware that the ark was not present in the second Temple.[30] This evidence seems to be cumulative and conclusive.

[29] For a quite different translation of this important and oft-cited passage, cf. Arnold, *op. cit.*, 73, and Budde's criticism thereof, *op. cit.*, 19 ff.

[29a] Cf. also II Mac. 5 15 f. and Josephus, *Antiquities*, XII, 5, 3.

[30] Cf. Lauterbach, "A Significant Controversy between the Sadducees and the Pharisees," *HUCA*, IV (1927), 184 and the references to Rabbinic literature cited by him there. This tradition that the ark originally stood upon the sacred stone, As-Sakhra, in the Temple of Solomon, that it had, in fact, been placed there by Joshua at Moses' command, and that it remained there until God became angry at Israel, and the Temple, i.e. undoubtedly the first Temple, was destroyed, whereupon the ark disappeared, passed over to Islam, and is recorded by As-Suyuti (cf. the translation of Reynolds, 108 and 118).

And other considerations of far-reaching significance for the history of the ark corroborate this conclusion. We may be sure that the ark was not present in the second Temple not merely because it had disappeared after the destruction of the first Temple, presumably having been carried away to Babylon as a trophy of victory, but for another reason as well, because, apparently, even before the destruction of the first Temple the ark had lost much of its original significance and had fallen somewhat into disrepute. For certainly, if the ark had continued to enjoy uninterruptedly the reputation which it enjoyed unquestionably as late as the time of David, and which is again attributed to it both in the Priestly Code and in the account of the dedication of Solomon's Temple in I Ki. 8, it goes without saying that Ezekiel must have made some provision for it in his plan of the rebuilt Temple, or have taken some cognizance of it, or at least of its absence. Instead he ignored it in the most offhand manner, quite as if to him the ark were something of no importance whatsoever, of which he did not even think, when he made his plans for the rebuilt Temple.

This too is the undeniable implication of Deut. 1. 33 and 42. For, as we have seen, v. 33 is directly dependent upon Num. 10. 33 b, and the reference to the ark and its leadership of Israel there has obviously been purposely suppressed here. This is the case also in v. 42. For this verse is, in turn, dependent upon Num. 14. 42 and 44. This latter verse says explicitly that when Israel sought to enter Palestine from the south, in the battle with the native inhabitants of the land the ark of the covenant of Yahwe and Moses did not move from the camp; they were therefore not present in the actual battle, and this, it is implied, and in fact actually stated in v. 42, was the reason for Israel's defeat. It is significant that in v. 44 the ark is mentioned first and Moses second, quite as if, what is undoubtedly the actual implication, the ark was the initiating force and Moses were but the secondary, dependent and attendant functionary. In other words, the ark is represented here as playing exactly the same rôle as in I Sam. 4–6, while Moses plays the rôle of attendant priest, just as do the sons of Eli in I Sam. 4. Just because of this specific rôle which the ark plays in v. 44, Moses is represented in v. 42 as warning Israel not to engage in battle, for Yahwe will not be present with them, and therefore they are sure to lose the battle; the presence of the ark in the army of Israel is synonymous with the presence of Yahwe there, and is the sure guarantee of victory, precisely as is implied in I Sam. 4. But in Deut. 1. 42 all mention of the ark is scrupulously suppressed, and only the colorless statement is left, that Yahwe will not be present with Israel in the battle, a statement which is, of course, the same as that of Num. 14. 42, but lacks entirely the amplifying and concrete statement of Num. 14. 44.[30a]

Undoubtedly the suppression of all reference to the ark by the author of Deut. 1 was not accidental, but was conscious and motivated by some definite reason. It is obvious that for the author of Deut. 1, who certainly lived and wrote in the early post-exilic period, i. e. in the early period of the second Temple, the ark did not enjoy the same reputation nor play the same rôle as it did in the early period of Israel's history, at least up to the time of David. Nay more, to him the ark must have been more than an object of indifferent significance; he must have had some strong and positive objection to it, for otherwise he would not have been so scrupulous in suppressing all reference to it. To him it must have seemed an object which did not accord at all with the pure, uncontaminated worship of Yahwe as he understood and interpreted it. Manifestly he put it in the same category as he put Hobab or Jethro and the "tent of meeting" and the oracle of Yahwe associated with it in the Kenite Document, all reference to which in the original narrative in Ex. 18, as we have seen,[31] he likewise suppressed in vv. 9–18 of this same chapter. Clearly he regarded the ark of the covenant of Yahwe, just as he regarded "the tent of meeting" and the oracle of Yahwe connected with it and the rôle of Hobab in relation thereto, as not of true and proper Yahwistic

---

[30a] Note also that according to Deut. 23. 15, likewise a post-exilic passage, Yahwe is present in the military camp of Israel, but, very significantly, here too His presence is not symbolized by the ark.

[31] "The Oldest Document of the Hexateuch," *HUCA*, IV (1927), 133, note 121.

origin. He must have looked upon them all as non-Yahwistic, and therefore as idolatrous, or at least as semi-idolatrous, in origin and character. This conception of them, and this alone, would account adequately for his manifestly purposed suppression of all reference to them. We can easily understand why he should have looked upon the "tent of meeting" and its oracle and upon Hobab's connection with them as non-Yahwistic; it was because of their Kenite, and to him therefore non-Israelite origin. Manifestly to him only that could be specifically Yahwistic which was distinctively Israelitish and of independent, unqualified Mosaic origin. But why should he have put the ark, specifically designated as "the ark of the covenant of Yahwe," in the same category? This question is, obviously, of great moment for this study. The answer will be given in due time.

It is clear from all this evidence that at a certain period in Israel's history the ark lost very much of its original significance and reputation, and came to be looked upon with little or no regard, at least by a considerable and influential group of Israel's religious thinkers and spokesmen. It is clear too that this decline in the reputation of the ark must have begun in the pre-exilic period, for otherwise Ezekiel would not have ignored it completely, nor would the author of Deut. 1, in the early post-exilic period, have suppressed all reference to it, nor the author of Jer. 3. 16, apparently, judging by the content of his message, a contemporary of, or else, at the latest, living but shortly after Zechariah, have pictured the ark as not present in the second Temple nor as being needed or desired there. This process of decline in the reputation of the ark, due probably to a growing conviction that it was not of true Yahwistic origin, must have begun during the period before the exile. Just when and how this conviction arose, we shall endeavor to determine.

Certainly the oldest Biblical references to the ark [32] agree absolutely in representing it as discharging two specific functions, that of choosing the way which it wished to go,

---

[32] Num. 10. 33 b, 35–36; 14. 44; Jud. 20. 27 b (perhaps a late, harmonistic gloss); I Sam. 46; II Sam. 6. 1–20; 11. 11; 15. 24–29.

and that of going into battle with the army of Israel and giving it victory over its enemies. Even II Sam. 15. 24-29 seems to imply that Zadok brought the ark from Jerusalem in order that it might accompany David upon his flight and thus assure him of ultimate victory over his rebellious son.[33] These two important functions the ark was able to discharge, all the evidence indicates, because of a positive divine power resident in it. And all these earliest sources agree in identifying this divine power with Yahwe. Of this more later.

The next Biblical reference to the ark in point of time, seemingly, is Deut. 10. 1-5. This passage is generally recognized as not an integral part of the original Deuteronomic Code, but as belonging to the secondary introduction thereto; it was therefore in all likelihood composed either during the exile or, what is more probable, in the early post-exilic period.[34] The passage represents Moses as making, at Yahwe's explicit command, a wooden ark or box, in which the second set of stone tablets with the ten commandments inscribed upon them, were to be deposited. This command Moses carried out punctiliously. It is certain, however, that this narrative is not original with this Deuteronomic writer, but was borrowed by him, perhaps with some characteristic modification, from a JE original. This fact is generally recognized by Biblical scholars. However, our present Biblical text contains no statement whatsoever of the original of this narrative. The usual claim of Biblical scholars is that this original account of the making of the ark by Moses must have stood in Ex. 33 immediately following v. 6, and that the ornaments of the people there mentioned must have provided the material from which the ark was made, or at least with which it was finished and decorated.[35] This hypothesis is plausible;

[33] Cf. Budde's very apposite discussion of the rôle of the ark in this passage; *op. cit.*, 24 f.
[34] This passage is unquestionably, as is generally recognized by Biblical scholars, not the work of the same Deuteronomic writer as the author of Deut. 1. Manifestly these two writers had different and even contradictory conceptions of and attitudes toward the ark.
[35] Cf. Gressmann, *op. cit.*, 22 ff.

certainly it has more to commend it than the parallel hypothesis that the "tent of meeting" was made from these ornaments.[36]

Actually the content of the narrative in Deut. 10. 1–5 seems to imply that the original narrative of the making of the ark by Moses, upon which it is dependent, stood rather in connection with Ex. 34. 1–5. For it tells of Yahwe's command to Moses to make the ark only in connection with and following the command to prepare the second set of stone tablets. Accordingly Moses makes the ark at the same time that he prepares the second tablets; he then ascends the mountain; Yahwe writes the ten commandments upon the second set of tablets and gives them back to Moses; Moses then returns to the camp and deposits the tablets in the ark, precisely as Yahwe had commanded him.[37] Just this must

[36] Cf. "The Oldest Document of the Hexateuch," *HUCA*, IV (1927), 119f.

[37] Deut. 10. 5 is of particular interest in this connection. It is self-apparent that the last words of the sentence, כאשר צוני יהוה, modify ואשם, and not שם ויהיו, immediately preceding. These two words therefore disturb the connection and are manifestly a late insertion into the text. But they must have been inserted for some particular purpose. They can be translated only, "and they are there," and not at all "and they were there," for this last would have no meaning whatsoever. But translated "and they are there," they can have only one specific meaning and purpose. They serve as a direct and positive affirmation, almost, it would seem, in the face of a doubt or question, that the tablets of the Ten Commandments were still present in the ark in the days, not merely of the original Deuteronomic author of this verse, but also of the late glossator who inserted these words here. These words, therefore, constitute an affirmation both that there was, supposedly, an ark in the Temple in the days of this glossator, and that, as he believed implicitly, the two tablets were still deposited in it. This is, of course, the point of view of the late Priestly writers. This points to quite a late date for this gloss.

This same conclusion holds true with I Ki. 8. 8b. There the words ויהיו שם עד היום הזה are manifestly a very late gloss, expressing the strong belief of the glossator, and intended also to convince his readers, that the staves of the ark, and therefore, of course, the ark itself were present in the innermost part of the Temple, even though they could not be seen by the people at large, or, for that matter, by any one other than the high-priest, when he entered the holy of holies once a year, on Yom Kippur. But again the fact that this glossator too seems to have felt compelled to insist in this manner that the ark was still present in the Temple in his day, even though it could not be seen, indicates that he must have had to contend with a prevalent and persistent doubt of this, a doubt founded in all likelihood upon actual fact.

have been the full content of the narrative of which Ex. 34. 1–5 was the introduction, and of which these five verses alone survive. The remainder must have been suppressed either by the J 2 editors who incorporated a portion of the Kenite Document, as we have seen, with the J narrative at just this particular point, although for what reason they should have felt obliged to suppress this statement it is difficult to imagine. Or, perhaps more probably, it may have been suppressed by later Priestly editors in favor of their own, quite different account of the making of the ark and of the occasion for it and the purpose which it was to serve.

But while it is almost certain that the author of Deut. 10. 1–5 must have found the JE narrative of the making of the ark linked with Ex. 34. 1–5, it is by no means impossible that it may have been connected originally with Ex. 33. 6 also. For, as we have said, the ornaments here mentioned could not possibly have been used for the making of the "tent of meeting," but they may well have been employed in the making of the ark. Moreover, as we have shown,[38] Ex. 33. 7–11, or rather the Kenite nucleus of this passage, originally stood in the Kenite Document in the position which is now occupied by the secondary narrative of Moses with the shining face, in 34. 29 ff., and was transposed from this position and amplified into its present form by late J 2 editors. Manifestly therefore the account of the making of the "tent of meeting" could have had no primary connection with the incident recorded in 33. 6.

But equally 33. 5 b–6 has no connection whatsoever with, and even contradicts absolutely the statement of v. 4, that the people did not put on their ornaments. Nor have vv. 5 b–6 any apparent connection with vv. 1–3, nor with the main content of Ex. 32. In fact they seem to parallel, and therefore to contradict, the narrative of Ex. 32. For 32. 2–3 tells that the people had already stripped of their ornaments and that out of them Aaron had made the golden calf. Seemingly 33. 5 b–6 stands by itself without any apparent connection with anything that precedes or anything

[38] "The Oldest Document of the Hexateuch," *HUCA*, IV (1927), 121 ff.

THE BOOK OF THE COVENANT

that follows. And yet these verses obviously imply that out of the ornaments which the people stripped off Moses did make something. Moreover, not only 33. 7–11, but also, as we have seen,[39] vv. 12–23 were inserted into their present position by the J 2 editors who incorporated fragments of the Kenite Document with J. Consequently before this incorporation Ex. 33. 5 b—6 probably stood in immediate juxtaposition to 34. 1—5, with its original account of the making of the ark; or perhaps better, since, as we have seen, 33. 5 b—6 has no immediate connection with either the J or E narratives, strata of which are present in Ex. 32 and 33. 1 b–4, 33. 5 b–6 may have been connected with an account of the making of the ark, which was originally not related at all to the narrative in 34. 1–5, and which came only through editorial processes to have connection with this narrative.

The import of all this is self-apparent. As is recognized by almost all modern Biblical scholars, Ex. 35. 1–Num. 10. 28 are the work of Priestly writers and are therefore late. Consequently in the pre-exilic period Num. 10. 29 must have followed immediately upon Ex. 34. 35. Therefore the reference to the ark in Num. 10. 33 b followed in the pre-exilic form of the Hexateuch almost immediately after Ex. 33. 5 b–6. In Num. 10. 33 b the ark appears very abruptly and even startlingly. It is inconceivable that this mention of the ark should not have been preceded by some account of its making by Moses. And if, as we contend, and as we shall endeavor to demonstrate conclusively, Num. 10. 33 b was originally a part of the Book of the Covenant, then it would follow that the Book of the Covenant must have contained likewise an account of the making of the ark, and that accordingly Ex. 33. 5 b–6, which has no apparent connection with anything that precedes it immediately, or with either the J or E codes proper, was likewise originally a part of C.[39 a]

Nay more, since the Book of the Covenant tells of the covenant established between Yahwe and Israel on the basis of a little code of " words," which were written by Moses

[39] *Ibid.*, 5 ff.
[39a] In v. 6 the last two words, מהר חורב, must be then the work of *RE*.

upon a scroll, and since this scroll was manifestly of primary
importance as the concrete record and witness of this
covenant, and therefore was presumably to be preserved most
carefully, it is but natural to assume that the Book of the
Covenant told of the making of the ark by Moses primarily
to be the place of deposit of the sacred scroll of the covenant.
This would mean, in turn, that the earliest form of the
tradition that the ark was the depository of the sacred record
of the covenant-" words," whether inscribed upon a scroll or
upon stones, was contained in C, that it was C which first
made of the old ark the ארון ברית יהוה, "the ark of the
covenant of Yahwe," and that the later accounts of J, E,
D and P developed out of this original. In such case then
it would follow that to the authors of C the ark discharged
two independent, and not easily reconcilable functions; on
the one hand, it was the depository of the scroll of the
covenant; on the other hand, it was, through the divine
power resident in it, the guide of Israel through the desert.
Manifestly this latter represents the older conception of the
power and function of the ark, while the former is a conception new, secondary, and likewise original with C. Impliedly it represents a modification by the authors of C of the
older conception of the ark, the beginning of that process
of reinterpretation of the character and functions of the ark
and of its eventual decline in reputation and regard, the
culmination of which we have found in Ezekiel's silence with
regard to the ark, in the suppression of all reference to it
in Deut. 1. 33 and 42 and in the judgment pronounced upon
it in Jer. 3. 16.

But it is equally certain that the late post-exilic period
witnessed a significant revival of the prestige of the ark
and of the rôle which it played in the religious theory and
practice of Israel. For in the Priestly Code the ark is
represented as the most holy object, the very center of
Israel's religious life.[40] And the question naturally arises,
why this revival? Moreover, since, as we have seen, the
evidence is quite conclusive that there was no ark in the

[40] Ex. 25. 10–22.

second Temple, at least not in the century more or less immediately following its erection in the early post-exilic period, it follows that the Priestly writers probably had no direct and authentic knowledge of the original ark and its appearance. Undoubtedly they had valuable traditions which guided them in their plan of reconstruction of the ark, and these traditions must have fixed for them its general shape and character. But in the two hundred years, more or less, that must have intervened between the actual disappearance of the ark and the oldest Priestly account of it, even the most reliable traditions had doubtless become somewhat vague, and ample room was left therefore for considerable exercise of the imagination on the part of Priestly writers and for modification of old traditions with regard to the form and function of the ark in order to conform to and further Priestly purpose in thus reviving the institution and prestige of the ark.

Now in the Priestly Code the ark discharges two distinct functions, each absolutely unrelated to the other, but also equally unrelated to the significant functions which the ark was believed to discharge in the earliest period of its history. On the one hand the ark is still the receptacle for the two stone tablets upon which the Ten Commandments are inscribed. And on the other hand, the ark is now the throne of Yahwe, upon which He sits in divine solitude and majesty in the holy of holies, having taken up His permanent residence in Israel's midst; and there He meets with Israel, or rather with Israel's divinely appointed representative, the high-priest, on the one occasion in the year when the latter was permitted to enter into the divine presence. Seemingly this representation of the ark as the divine throne is something new and original with the Priestly Code, and does not accord at all with the earlier conceptions of the ark. Certainly the ark is not depicted as the divine throne or seat of Yahwe in a single authentic passage earlier than the Priestly Code or writings dependent upon this. There is therefore not the slightest ground for regarding this conception of the ark as of any great antiquity and historicity.

Moreover, it is clear that actually this conception of the ark as the throne of Yahwe is the only significant rôle which it plays in the scheme of the Priestly Code, and that its other role, as the receptacle of the tablets of the Decalogue, is of no practical significance whatever in this scheme, and is but a concession to or survival from older tradition.[41]

[41] In the Priestly Code the most general name for the ark is ארון העדות, "the ark of testimony." This name is, of course, derived from the traditional presence of the two tablets with the Ten Commandments upon them in the ark. The tablets themselves are called לחת העדת, "the tablets of testimony" (Ex. 31. 18; 32. 15; 34. 29), while the Ten Commandments inscribed upon them are designated as "the testimony," העדת (Ex. 25. 16, 21). The same term likewise designates both the ark and its contents (Ex. 16. 34; 30. 36; Num. 17. 19, 25). Consequently, because of the presence of the ark, with the stone tablets inside, in the sanctuary, the latter is called repeatedly either משכן העדת (Ex. 38. 21; Num. 1. 50, 53; 10. 11) or אהל העדת (Num. 9. 15; 17. 22, 23; 18. 2; II Chron. 26. 6), and the veil before the ark, separating the holy of holies from the rest of the tabernacle, is called פרכת העדת, "the veil of testimony" (Lev. 24. 3). The term עדות in these various combinations is found only in P or in Biblical writings later than P and composed under Priestly influence (cf., for example, Ps. 19. 8, where עדות is used in parallelism with תורה). It implies, of course, that the ark, or, more exactly, the two tablets present in the ark, upon which the Ten Commandments, the basis of Yahweh's covenant with Israel, were inscribed, were to bear testimony, testimony, of course, to the eternal covenant which Yahwe had established with Israel, or at least to the character of Yahwe's peculiar relations with Israel.

But while the term עדות, used either independently or in these various combinations, is found only in P, and with such frequency that it follows that the idea which it conveys must be basic in P, none the less it is certain, on the one hand, that the idea itself is not original in P, and, on the other hand, that in P it is used in an altogether conventional sense, and that the P writers had no adequate understanding of its true implication. For, were the ark, or rather the stone tablets within the ark, to serve as testimony of Yahwe's relations with Israel, it would follow that they must have been exhibited to Israel on occasion, either at some regular moment or moments during the year, or else whenever the need warranted. In just this manner the hairs from the beard of the prophet, kept in a silver case in the Mosque of Omar in Jerusalem, are exhibited on each recurring 27th of Ramâḍân, the traditional lêlatu-l-Qadr (Canaan, "Mohammedan Saints and Sanctuaries in Palestine," JPOS, IV [1924], 82, note 1). But just such exhibit of the tablets of testimony is not only forbidden by the Priestly conception of and attitude toward them, but likewise it was in all likelihood made impossible by a practical consideration.

For to the Priestly theologians the ark and its contents were sacrosanct. They stood in the holy of holies, which could never be entered by a lay

V

The Three Periods in the History of the Ark

This evidence establishes firmly that there were three distinct periods in the history of the ark and of the functions Israelite, nor even by an ordinary priest or Levite, but only by the high-priest, and that only once a year, and only when he was enveloped in an artificial cloud of incense, prescribed purposely in order that he might not see too much during his very brief sojourn within the holy of holies (cf. Lauterbach, " A Significant Controversy between the Sadducees and the Pharisees," *HUCA*, IV [1927], 173-205). In other words, although the ark and its contents were to serve as testimony unto Israel, they never were and never could be exhibited to Israel in order to discharge this function. And in the second place, even had this function been permissible, it would have been exceedingly difficult, if not altogether impossible, because of the presence of the golden *kapporet* upon the ark. It is true that nowhere is it stated that the opening of the ark was from above, and not from one of its sides, nor is there any direct evidence pointing to a definite answer to this question. Yet on the one hand, the presence of the staves, by which the ark was carried, would seem to preclude the possibility of the opening of the ark being in at least its two long sides, and on the other hand, the association in the detailed description of the ark in Ex. 25. 10-22 of the depositing of the two tablets of testimony in the ark and the placing of the *kapporet* on top of the ark seems to imply that the tablets were deposited in the ark through an opening in the top, and not on the side, and that immediately after the tablets had been thus deposited, the *kapporet* was placed upon this opening as a cover. This, too, is the implication of the statement in Ex. 40. 3 that the *kapporet* covered, or stopped up the opening (וסכת; cf. Torczyner, *op. cit.*, 239-247) of the ark. It is likewise implied in the etymological significance of the term *kapporet*; for whether " to cover " (and thereby at the same time " to conceal ") be a primary or a secondary meaning of the stem כפר (*ibid.*, 246 and Gesenius-Buhl, 359), unquestionably the fundamental meaning of *kapporet* was " covering "; and this meaning it could have best if conceived of, not merely as resting upon, but as actually filling up the opening in the top of the ark through which the contents had been inserted. But in such case the tablets of testimony within the ark could have been exhibited to the people, and thereby alone have discharged their function as testimony of the covenant, only if the heavy golden *kapporet* were removed. And not only would this have been a difficult procedure, but it would have been wholly incompatible with the dominant conception of the Priestly Code, that the *kapporet* was the seat of Yahwe, where He sat permanently enthroned in the midst of Israel.

It is clear, therefore, that the Priestly writers, despite the frequency of their use of the term, employed עדות only in a conventional sense, and with little understanding of or feeling for its literal meaning. Manifestly the conception of the Ten Commandments as the testimony of Yahwe's covenant with Israel was not original with them, but must have been borrowed by them from some older source or tradition.

which it was thought to discharge. In the period before the composition of the Book of the Covenant the ark was conceived of as leading Israel upon the march and selecting the way which it should go and of going into battle with the armies of Israel and giving it victory over its enemies. These functions it was thought to discharge because of a certain divine power resident in it. The presence of this divine power in the ark caused it to be popularly regarded as a deity, or perhaps better, as containing a deity, or if not this,

In all likelihood they coined the term עֵדוּת, for the ending ת probably points to late, Aramaic influence in the formation of the word. The natural forerunner of the term in classical Hebrew was, in all likelihood, עֵדָה, or in the plural, as generally used, עֵדוֹת. This word is used by Deuteronomic writers (Deut. 4. 45; 6. 17, 20) as one of the common terms for law, although it does not refer to the Ten Commandments specifically. In Ps. 132. 12, however, it is coordinated with ברית. Etymologically the term עדה or עדות represents the laws as the testimony or testimonies of Yahwe's relations with Israel. And while it is true that Deuteronomy does not apply this term specifically to the Decalogue, none the less it is difficult to conceive of the origin of the term other than in relation to the Ten Commandments regarded as the primary testimony of Yahwe's covenant with Israel. That this idea is characteristically Deuteronomic is proved by the injunction of Deut. 31. 26, that the Levitical priests shall deposit the " book of the law," i.e. Deuteronomy, represented as the legislation secondary to and supplementing the primary legislation of the Ten Commandments (cf. Deut. 4. 1–13 with 14 ff.) beside the ark as a witness unto Israel. Manifestly therefore to these Deuteronomic writers the ark itself was primarily the place of deposit of the basic testimony of Yahwe's covenant with Israel. Accordingly Deuteronomic writers likewise represented Samuel as depositing the book or scroll, in which he had recorded for Israel the plan of royal government sanctioned by Yahwe, " before Yahwe," i.e. unquestionably before the ark (I Sam. 10. 25; for לפני יהוה in Deuteronomic writings equivalent to " before the ark," cf. Josh. 4. 13; 6. 8), forgetful of the fact that, according to the older tradition, the ark was at this time no longer in Samuel's custody. This motif Priestly writers seem to have borrowed from their Deuteronomic forerunners, when they represented various sacred objects as deposited beside the ark; cf. Ex. 16. 34; Num. 17. 19, 25.

Furthermore, it is altogether probable that the JE original of the Deuteronomic narrative of Moses' making the ark and depositing the two tablets in it, also conceived of the tablets as deposited there, not merely for safekeeping, but that they might serve as permanent witness of Yahwe's covenant with Israel. And it is quite probable that this was the conception even of C, that in it too the Book of the Covenant was represented as deposited in the ark, not only for safekeeping, but also to serve as a witness of Yahwe's covenant with Israel, made upon the basis of the " words " contained in the Book.

then at least as a kind of tribal or national fetish or cult-object.

In the period beginning apparently with the composition of the Book of the Covenant and continuing through that of secondary strata of the Book of Deuteronomy, the ark came to be regarded generally as the depository of the record of the laws basic to Yahwe's covenant with Israel, whether written down in the scroll of the Book of the Covenant, or inscribed upon the two tablets of stone of J, E, D and P. Moreover, as we have seen, toward the end of this period, the real, historical ark had not only disappeared in all likelihood, but it had also forfeited so much of its earlier reputation for power and sanctity that its absence was not even looked upon with regret.

And finally, in the third period of its history, the period represented by the Priestly Code, and not even by the earlier strata thereof, the Holiness and Torah strata, but rather by the later strata, the Grundschrift, so-called, and secondary strata of this, the ark, although traditionally and conventionally still thought of as the depository of the two stone tablets of the Ten Commandments, was none the less now regarded primarily as the throne of Yahwe, upon which, in the holy of holies, He sat permanently enthroned in the midst of Israel.

Manifestly these three conceptions of the ark and its functions have little or nothing in common, but represent three distinct developments more or less exclusive of and antagonistic to each other. These three conceptions of the ark and its functions go hand in hand with three different stages in the evolution of the conception of Yahwe in Israel. Unquestionably these different and evolving conceptions of the ark and its functions were the offshoots of just this changing and evolving conception of Yahwe.

A

THE SECOND PERIOD

As we have said, the second period in the history of the ark began apparently with the composition of the Book of the Covenant. Certainly as late as the reign of David the ark was still popularly regarded in its old light, was still thought to go into battle with the armies of Israel and give them victory. For this reason the ark is represented in II Sam. 11. 11 as accompanying Joab and the army in the siege of Rabbat Ammon,[42] and for the same reason, as we have seen, Zadok and Ebiathar brought out the ark to accompany David upon his flight before Absalom.[43] How long this old conception of the ark and its functions may have continued to hold sway in popular thought, it is impossible to determine for lack of evidence bearing upon the rôle of the ark in the period intervening between the reign of David and the composition of the Book of the Covenant.[44]

During this period, however, the conception of Yahwe and His worship by Israel underwent serious and far-reaching modification. The Temple at Jerusalem was erected, to serve as the national sanctuary of Yahwe, now conceived of as

[42] Cf. Budde's very pertinent discussion of this passage (*op. cit.*, 21 ff.) in refutation of Arnold's interpretation of it.
[43] II Sam. 15. 24 ff. Cf. also Budde's discussion of this passage (*op. cit.*, 24 ff.), again in refutation of Arnold.
[44] An inference with regard to this question may perhaps be drawn from a comparison of Num. 14. 42 and 44 with Deut. 1. 42 ff. In the former account of Israel's battle with the native inhabitants of southern Palestine, the ark, symbolizing the presence of Yahwe, does not go into battle with Israel's army, and in consequence Israel is defeated. But, as we have already seen, this entire *motif* has been suppressed in the Deuteronomic version of this incident, and the ark is not mentioned. Since Num. 14. 40 ff. is unquestionably J, we may perhaps infer that J at least preserved a lively reminiscence of the function of the ark as the symbol of Yahwe's presence and the guarantor of victory in battle, but that by Deuteronomic times this had either been forgotten completely or else, as we have suggested, a conscious attempt was made to root out this tradition of the ark from the religious belief of the people. Certainly the rôle played by the ark in the narratives of the crossing of the Jordan and the conquest of Jericho, in Josh. 3, 4 and 6, is a late and artificial reminiscence of the old conception of the ark as the divine power which indicated the road which Israel should take, on this occasion through the hitherto concealed and therefore entirely unknown bed of the Jordan (cf. 3. 4), and which likewise gave Israel victory in battle. These passages are all the work of late Deuteronomic and Priestly redactors (cf. Steuernagel's analysis of these chapters in his *Commentary*, in the Nowack *Handkommentar* series). They have therefore no independent value whatever for the determination of the history of the ark.

Israel's national god. We have seen [45] that the religious reformation in the reign of Asa was, in all likelihood, directed in part against the Temple at Jerusalem, still a comparatively recent institution in 899 B.C., and, in opposition to the Temple, aimed to revive the old "tent of meeting," intimately associated with the early religious history of Moses, the tribe of Judah and the Kenites, as the only proper and divinely appointed place and medium of worship of Yahwe by Israel. In this respect, of course, the reformation failed and the Temple at Jerusalem continued to be looked upon as the center of true Yahwe worship in Israel.

But that the Temple at Jerusalem was regarded at this time as the actual residence of Yahwe, is open to serious question. Certainly Elijah, at about 870 B.C., did not look upon the Temple in this light, but, in full accord with the principles which animated the reformation of Asa, a generation before his time, he thought of Yahwe as still dwelling upon the mountain in the desert, where those tribes which had escaped from Egypt under the leadership of Moses had first come into contact and entered into covenant with Him. It is obviously a matter of prime importance for the study of the history of the ark to determine just when the concept did arise that Yahwe had taken up His sole and permanent residence in the Temple.

At first glance the question seems simple of answer. Amos 1. 2 represents Yahwe as roaring from Zion and sending forth His voice from Jerusalem. The authenticity of this verse has been doubted by some scholars, but upon altogether uncertain grounds. Certainly the verse conceives of the Temple at Jerusalem as Yahwe's abiding-place. Is. 8. 18 b is even more explicit, for it speaks of Yahwe as "He who dwells upon Mt. Zion." The authenticity of this phrase too has been questioned by some scholars, but again their argument is inconclusive. And it is admitted by all that the contrast between the waters of Siloah and the Euphrates, i. e. between Yahwe and Assyria as the objects of Israel's faith and reliance, would be entirely without point, did it not imply a direct relationship

---

[45] "The Oldest Document of the Hexateuch," *HUCA*, IV (1927), 123 ff.

between Yahwe and the Pool of Siloah, just below the Temple Mount, such a relationship as the sojourn of Yahwe in the Temple would suggest. This is probably the implication of Is. 28. 16 also. Likewise in Is. 1. 12 appearing before Yahwe in the Temple and treading down His courts, unquestionably imply the residence of Yahwe in the Temple at Jerusalem, provided of course that, as seems to be the case, the prophet has in mind only the Temple at Jerusalem, and not local shrines as well. Apparently too the popular expression. "Is not Yahwe in our midst?," in Mic. 3. 11, implies His residence in the Temple at Jerusalem; and this seems to be confirmed by the designation of Zion as "the mountain of the house" in the next verse.

But this seems to exhaust the list of passages in pre-Jeremian prophetic literature which point directly to the residence of Yahwe in the Temple at Jerusalem.[46] And it is

[46] I Ki. 8. 12f. might be cited as an exception to this statement, and particularly in the fuller form of the verses as emended according to LXX. It is usually contended by scholars that these verses are very old, the fragment of an ancient poem. Unquestionably in comparison with the setting, partly Deuteronomic and partly Priestly, in which these two verses occur, they are old. The fact too that, as the LXX version states, the poem, of which these verses are a fragment, was included originally in an old collection of poems, either a so-called "Book of Song," as the LXX text reads, or, as has been suggested by scholars, the Book of Yashar, points to a certain relative antiquity for the poem. But that the poem was actually of very great antiquity, and particularly that it actually goes back to Solomon, is doubtful. In the fuller form of the verses, as emended according to LXX, a contrast is drawn between Yahwe and the sun. Yahwe has set the sun in the heaven, but He Himself has chosen to dwell in darkness. This last, of course, refers to the concept that Yahwe dwelt within the $d^e bir$ of the Temple. The contrast between Yahwe and the sun is indeed strange and significant. Why it should have been made, and particularly at the time of the erection of the Temple, or even shortly thereafter, it is difficult to imagine. Yahwe is here represented as the lord and creator of the sun; the sun is His agent or instrument. Such a concept is not only not early, but it has a decidedly theological ring. We shall see shortly that as the result of natural, syncretistic processes, after the settlement of Israel in Palestine, Yahwe was gradually invested with the attributes of a solar deity, but that, beginning with the Deuteronomic reformation, a systematic attempt was made to divest Him of all solar attributes, and with this, of course, to represent Him as a truly universal deity, therefore the creator and lord of the sun as well as of all other phenomena of the universe. These verses smack so

difficult indeed to avoid the impression that this list is singularly small and inconclusive. For had the idea that Yahwe actually dwelt solely and permanently in the Temple been firmly rooted in the belief of the people in the days of Amos, Hosea and particularly Isaiah, there would have been innumerable occasions to refer to it explicitly. Consequently the manifest paucity of these references raises a serious doubt with regard to the degree to which this idea had at this time spread and taken deep root in the belief and practice of the people.

And this doubt is confirmed by a number of very serious considerations. Is. 29. 3 pictures Yahwe as camping about Jerusalem and besieging it; and only with difficulty can this picture be made to conform to the idea of Yahwe dwelling permanently within the Temple. Is. 31. 4 is even more explicit and significant in this regard, for it describes Yahwe as descending to wage war against Mount Zion. Necessarily we must ask, descending from where? And to this question Mic. 1. 2, 3, 12 furnish the clear answer; Yahwe comes forth from His heavenly temple or palace and descends upon the earth, so that the mountains melt beneath Him and the valleys are cleft asunder; and with Him evil descends against the gate of Jerusalem. This too seems to be the implication of Hos. 5. 14, that Yahwe will desert Israel and Judah and return to His place, i.e., presumably, heaven. Moreover, with significant frequency and regularity the J code represents Yahwe as coming down to earth to establish contact with mortals, whether it be to observe the Tower of Babel and to scatter the people and confound their speech,[47] or to confer with Moses in the sight of all the people.[48] Manifestly the implication here is that Yahwe dwells in heaven and descends

strongly of this Deuteronomic theology that it is practically impossible to ascribe an earlier origin to them. They apply perfectly to the second Temple and its dedication, but not at all to the first Temple. We can not therefore interpret these two verses as indicative of an early, pre-Deuteronomic belief that Yahwe actually resided in the Temple at Jerusalem.

[47] Gen. 11. 5, 7; cf. Gen. 18. 21; Ex. 3. 8.
[48] Ex. 19. 11, 18, 20; 33. 9; 34. 5; Num. 11. 25; 12. 5; LXX to Deut. 31. 15.

only occasionally to commune with mortals, and especially with Israel, either to reveal His law and will unto them or to visit His wrath upon them.

Here then we have two apparently contradictory and mutually exclusive concepts of Yahwe's dwelling-place, both seemingly current in the same period, and both even finding forceful expression in the utterances of the same two prophets, Isaiah and Micah. Is it possible that these two conflicting concepts were satisfactorily harmonized in the belief of the people; in other words, could the people have conceived of Yahwe at one and the same time as dwelling in heaven and likewise in the Temple at Jerusalem in their very midst? Is. 6 suggests the answer, and in a manner of utmost significance for this study.

This stirring vision represents the young prophet as beholding Yahwe seated upon a lofty throne in the Temple,[49] surrounded by a number of attendant angels, or winged, divine creatures. It is not immediately clear whether the narrative implies that Yahwe dwells permanently in the Temple, though ordinarily invisible to mortals, and only on this one particular occasion permits Himself to be seen by the young prophet, or whether it implies that Yahwe had just entered the Temple when the prophet beheld Him. The former is the traditional and almost universally accepted interpretation. In fact the latter seems not to have occurred to any one. Yet a moment's thought shows that the picture here of Yahwe in the Temple is not at all that which is general in Biblical literature. Yahwe sits enthroned here apparently not in the innermost recesses of the Temple, in the *debir* or the "holy of holies," in solitary grandeur, but out in the body of the Temple, so that the train of His robe fills the entire Temple.

Moreover, the reference to the quaking threshold seems to imply that Yahwe had just passed over it through the door of the Temple; therefore the threshold still quakes; for

---

[49] For a full and clear discussion of the question whether Isaiah saw Yahwe enthroned in the Temple at Jerusalem or in the heavenly temple, as Jewish tradition and also a few modern commentators would have it, and convincing proof that it was the Temple at Jerusalem, cf. Gray, *Isaiah*, I, 105 f. (*International Critical Commentary* series).

the passage can scarcely mean that the threshold quaked permanently because Yahwe dwelt within the Temple. Manifestly the picture here implies one of two things, either that Yahwe had just come forth into the body of the Temple from the "holy of holies" in the innermost part of the Temple, in which He resided permanently, or that He had just entered the Temple from without, coming in over the threshold, which quaked at His majestic passing; in this latter case coming down, of course, from heaven where He was thought to have His true and permanent abode. There can not be the least doubt as to which of these two implications is correct. Nowhere in Biblical literature or in ancient Jewish tradition do we find the slightest trace of a belief that Yahwe ever came forth from the "holy of holies" to take His place in the body of the Temple. But we have had a number of references in Biblical writings of this very period speaking of Yahwe's descent from heaven. And the J code in particular tells explicitly of Yahwe's descent from heaven either on the top of Mt. Sinai, to reveal the Decalogue, or at the very door of the tabernacle to commune with Moses. Unquestionably the implication of this narrative is that Yahwe has just descended from heaven, accompanied by His train of heavenly attendants, and has just entered the Temple through the open gate, so that the threshold is still quaking at the moment when the prophet beholds Yahwe.

And if this interpretation of this interesting narrative be correct, it suggests the answer to our question as to how it was possible to conceive of Yahwe as dwelling in heaven and on occasion descending therefrom, yet at the same time being present in the Temple at Jerusalem in such manner that the people could believe that Yahwe was in their midst, that Amos could speak of Yahwe as roaring from Zion and sending forth His voice from Jerusalem, and that Isaiah could personify Yahwe as the waters of Siloah. It seems to imply that Yahwe's true dwelling-place was in heaven, but that upon some regular annual occasion He descended therefrom and entered the Temple and there He sat enthroned for a time surrounded by His heavenly host. And besides this He could, upon special occasions, descend from heaven, either to commune with His people through His chosen servants or to visit His divine wrath upon them. What could have been the regular, annual occasion of Yahwe's descent from heaven and entrance into the Temple?

The chapter apparently gives not the slightest indication of the particular occasion of this vision. The natural and customary inference is that it was upon no particular occasion, but merely a chance occurrence that the young Isaiah, happening in the most ordinary manner to be in the Temple, beheld this august vision. Yet it is self-evident that the entire incident has more point and force if it is thought to have happened upon a certain particular occasion, an occasion directly related in some way to the content of the vision and its import to the youthful prophet, rather than if it had happened at a chance, insignificant moment.[50]

[50] It is self-evident that I Ki. 22. 19 ff. presents a close parallel to Is. 6. In both the prophet sees a vision of Yahwe enthroned and attended by heavenly beings. And in both passages a message comes to the prophet from the Deity, designed to bring about the destruction of the object against whom the vision is directed, in the one case Ahab, the king, in the other case the entire nation of Israel. This parallelism is so close and striking that it is impossible to escape the conclusion of direct dependence of the one upon the other. Nor can there be any question that Is. 6 is the original and I Ki. 22. 19 ff. the dependent vision. This would imply, of course, that I Ki. 22. 19 ff. being dependent upon Is. 6, must be later than 740 B.C., and in all likelihood later by not a few years; accordingly it must be secondary in I Ki. 22, as quite a number of authoritative Biblical scholars have maintained (cf. Kittel, *Commentary*, in Nowack's *Handkommentar* series, 174). This conclusion is corroborated by one consideration of much importance for this study. Does I Ki. 22. 19 ff., like Is. 6, envision Yahwe enthroned in the Temple at Jerusalem or in heaven? Unquestionably the latter. For, on the one hand, it would have been altogether incongruous for an official, professional prophet of the Northern Kingdom during the reign of Ahab to have envisioned Yahwe enthroned in the Temple at Jerusalem. Moreover, a moment's thought shows that this is no real vision, actually beheld by the prophet with ordinary sight, as that in Is. 6 undoubtedly was, but instead it is either a literary, fictitious vision, or, at the most, a psychical vision, something which the prophet saw, or believed that he saw, not with his physical, but only with his mind's eye, as it were. This is proved by the preceding vision in v. 17, where the prophet also sees, and this certainly only in a psychical state, all Israel leaderless and scattered. From this it is clear that the dependence of I Ki. 22. 19 ff. upon Is. 6, while real, is so only in external

THE BOOK OF THE COVENANT

In a very interesting passage the Talmud [51] records the surprising fact that the Temple at Jerusalem was so located and built that on the two annual equinoctial days the first rays of the rising sun would shine directly through the eastern gate. Considerable evidence, to be gathered from a great variety of sources, shows that this eastern gate was kept fast closed all through the year, but was opened on these two particular days for just this especial purpose. The entrance of these first rays of the rising sun upon the two equinoctial days through the eastern gate and directly into the very heart of the Temple, was thought to symbolize the coming of Yahwe and His presence within the Temple, at least on those days. For this reason the day of the fall equinox was celebrated in ancient Israel as the New Year's Day. It was accordingly the day when Yahwe was thought to sit in the midst of His heavenly court and administer justice and decide the destinies of Israel, and perhaps of other nations also, for the ensuing year.

It was the coming of the first rays of the rising sun on the mornings of the two equinoctial days, and especially of the fall equinox, that was known as the coming of the $k^ebod\ Yahwe$, "the glory of Yahwe." Ezek. 43. 2 ff. gives the most concrete picture of this. On the New Year's Day the prophet sees in his vision the $k^ebod\ Yahwe$, or as he calls it there, the $k^ebod\ {}^eloh̊e\ Yisra'el$, coming from the east, with a sound like the noise of mighty waters, and as it comes along the earth is lit up by its radiance.[52] He sees

circumstances in the framework of the vision, and not at all in its inner concepts and content. This consideration likewise makes it certain that Yahwe is here envisioned enthroned, not in the Temple at Jerusalem, as in Is. 6, but in heaven. This is, of course, a concept frequently alluded to in late Biblical passages, such as Is. 66. 1; Job. 2. 1. This fact too corroborates the conclusion that I Ki. 22. 19 ff. is late.

[51] Jer. Erubin, V, 22 c.

[52] מכבודן. For כבוד = " radiance," cf. Is. 10. 16 f., where כבדו stands, on the one hand, in parallelism with אור ישראל, and on the other hand, in contrast with יקר ביקוד אש; Zech. 2. 9, where Yahwe declares that He will be a wall of fire (חומת אש) round about the city (of course in order to protect it against danger from without) and radiance (כבד) within (i.e. shining benignantly and without harm upon its inhabitants); Is. 60. 1 ff., " Arise, shine, for thy light (i.e. Yahwe)

it approach the Temple and enter by the eastern gate and take up its permanent residence within the Temple. Thereis come, and the *kᵉbod Yahwe* has risen (like the sun, זרח) upon thee. Behold, darkness covereth the earth, and deep darkness the nations; but upon thee doth Yahwe rise (like the sun, יזרח), and His radiance (or His *kabod*, i.e. the *kᵉbod Yahwe*, which amounts to the same thing) is revealed (or hath revealed itself) unto thee. And nations shall go toward thy light (i.e. Yahwe), and kings toward thy radiant sunrise" (literally, "toward the radiance or brilliance of thy sunrising"). The parallelism here shows clearly that this is but a poetic equivalent for the *kᵉbod Yahwe*, i.e. for Yahwe represented by the first rays of the rising sun. Moreover, the background of the picture here is the celebration of the interesting ceremonies of the *simḥat bet hašo'ebah*, in connection with the Succoth-festival (cf. Sukkah, V). Until the time of Ezra, and even for a time thereafter, this was the old New Year's Day celebration (cf. my "The Three Calendars of Ancient Israel," *HUCA*, I [1924], 22–58). Unquestionably the sunrise here referred to, correlated with the manifestation of Yahwe's presence, is the sunrise upon the day of the fall equinox, the New Year's Day. Is. 59. 19 likewise correlates the radiance of Yahwe, or the *kᵉbod Yahwe*, with the east, the place of sunrise, while at the same time, and singularly enough, it correlates the "name of Yahwe," likewise a manifestation of the Deity, with the west. Furthermore, Ex. 16. 10 (belonging to P2, and therefore coming from the late post-exilic period) represents Israel, but recently emerged from Egypt and marching eastward through the desert, looking towards the desert, i.e. of course towards the east, and beholding the *kᵉbod Yahwe*.

In all these passages כבוד, standing by itself, has unquestionably the meaning "radiance," or else, used in the technical term *kᵉbod Yahwe*, is obviously associated with the radiance of the first rays of the rising sun upon the day of the fall equinox, the New Year's Day. Consequently in this compound term כבוד could be best and most literally translated "radiance" of Yahwe. Accordingly we must translate Is. 6. 3 (and with it, of course, the dependent passage Ps. 72. 19) "the whole earth is filled with His radiance." Likewise Ps. 57. 6, 12; 108. 6, "Be high above the heavens, O God; over all the earth be Thy radiance"; and Ps. 113. 4, "Exalted above all nations is Yahwe; His radiance is over the heavens." Also in Is. 4. 5 כבוד must either be translated "radiance," or, perhaps better be regarded as a contraction of the fuller expression *kᵉbod Yahwe*; for here too the background of the picture is the characteristic Priestly representation of the *kᵉbod Yahwe*, a flaming apparition, visible to Israel at night, but in form subdued, and therefore harmless to the vision, either by the darkness of the night, or, as here, because enveloped in smoke, but during the day enveloped in the cloud, and therefore itself invisible to Israel (cf. Ex. 24. 15–18; 40. 34–38). Perhaps also in Is. 24. 23 כבוד should be translated "radiance," and the picture here be contrasted with that of Ex. 24. 10. Not improbably also in Is. 30. 27 לְבָדּ should be translated "radiant" or "gleaming." The passage is difficult indeed, and neither ancient versions nor modern commentators have been able to make anything satisfactory out of it. For כבד משאה LXX seems to have read בכבוד אמרת שמתי. And since Targum paraphrases the end of the same verse אכלא כאשא וטימריה,

fore the prophet is charged to see that henceforth the eastern gate is kept closed forever, i. e., never again to be reopened, as formerly, on the two annual equinoctial days. The old ceremony of the opening of the gates for the day, and the solemn closing of them at the end of the day's ceremonies, the prophet very manifestly seeks to abrogate. This is, of course, because he is fully aware of the original idolatrous rites connected with the worship of the sun at this open eastern gate,[53] and in order to counteract the impression that they have aught to do with the pure worship of Yahwe. But he has also a second motive in thus prescribing that this eastern gate must be kept closed forever; thereby he symbolizes concretely to the people of Israel that Yahwe is now actually dwelling permanently in their midst, that He is there, in the Temple, no longer merely upon the New Year's Day, but throughout the entire year, at all times, permanently.

But while Ezekiel thus makes extensive use of the idea and ceremonial of the coming of the $k^e bod\ Yahwe$ into the Temple[54] at Jerusalem on the New Year's Day, it is by no

we must infer that LXX probably understood כבוד here as meaning "radiance," like that of a consuming fire. Certainly the "light of the seven days," in v. 26 refers to the illuminations in the Temple and throughout the entire city, and in fact through the whole land of Palestine, during the seven days of the ceremonies of the *simḥaṯ beṯ haso'ebah*, i. e. the seven days of the Succoth-festival; and v. 29 makes explicit and rather detailed reference to these same ceremonies. Probably therefore, whatever be the actual meaning of v. 27, the background is also that of these same festival rites, with their association with the first rays of the rising sun upon the day of the fall equinox and the consequent coming of the $k^e bod\ Yahwe$. לְפָנֵי here is apparently in parallelism with בָּא, and therefore has been traditionally vocalized as a participle. All this evidence points to the probability of the translation "radiant."

In this connection it is interesting and significant to note that Charlier ("Ein astronomischer Beitrag zur Exegese des Alten Testaments," *ZDMG*, 58 [1904], 392 f.), working upon altogether independent grounds, arrived at the same conclusion that the $k^e bod\ Yahwe$ must be correlated with the first rays of the rising sun upon the days of the equinox.

[53] Cf. Ezek. 8. 16 ff. and Sukkah, V, 4.

[54] This entire subject of the $k\ bod\ Yahwe$ and its coming into the Temple through the eastern gate on the New Year's Day is one of exceeding importance for the history of the religion of Israel. But, as the few points discussed in note 52 indicate, it is entirely too vast in extent and too complex to be treated here in detail. This must await another occasion.

means original with him. Ezek. 8. 16 ff. proves that this was an old ceremony in the Temple at Jerusalem, probably but loosely coordinated with the worship of Yahwe. What Ezekiel, although perhaps half unconsciously, aimed to do, was, as we have just intimated, to divest the ceremony of its most obvious and objectionable non-Yahwistic elements and give it a proper and legitimate place in the Yahwe-Temple and cult.

The antiquity of the institution is further attested by the realization that it constituted likewise the basis of the picture in Is. 6 and the occasion of the young prophet's vision in the Temple. There too we have Yahwe and His *kabod*, His radiance, filling the entire world. He is seated upon a high throne in the Temple, surrounded by the seraphim, winged, angelic creatures, manifestly the forerunners of the cherubim of Ezekiel. Probably, as the name *serafim* indicates, they were conceived of as fiery beings, shining with a radiance comparable to, but no doubt inferior to, and perhaps emanating by reflection from Yahwe. Here too, just as in all accounts of the manifestation of the *kebod Yahwe*, the sanctuary is filled with smoke, or, what amounts to the same thing, with cloud.[55] And here too, just as in other accounts, the prophet fears that he must die, for he has beheld Yahwe; and ordinarily for a mortal to gaze upon Yahwe, even in the form of the *kebod Yahwe*, meant death.[56]

And what is Yahwe doing here in the Temple on this New Year's Day? Apparently judging the peoples and pronouncing their destinies for the ensuing year. For when, in v. 8, the prophet, his lips purified by the coal from off the altar, is made to hear clearly and to understand the full import of what Yahwe is saying, the words are, "Whom shall I send, and who will go for us?," i. e. who shall be our agent, to carry out our plan and thus fulfill the destiny of Israel appointed for that year? And what this destiny is, is stated clearly in vv. 9 ff., the complete destruction of the nation and desolation

[55] Ex. 40. 35; I Ki. 8. 10f.; Is. 4. 5; Ezek. 10. 4.
[56] Cf. Gen. 32. 31; Ex. 33. 20; Num. 16. 20, 35; Jud. 13. 22; also my "Moses with the Shining Face," *HUCA*, II (1925), 1–27.

of the land. But since, in accordance with the prophetic teaching of the day,[56a] before Israel might be destroyed by Yahwe it must be warned of its impending doom and summoned to repent, this shall be the mission of the ardent, young devotee. But likewise, since Israel's destiny of doom has been fixed by Yahwe and His divine court, and its destruction is therefore inevitable, the mission of the prophet must be fruitless, even though it be indispensable; accordingly he must speak to a people fat of heart, heavy of ear and sealed of eye, a people therefore which can not repent and return to Yahwe and thus escape its sentence of doom.

Unquestionably the background of this picture represents Yahwe seated in the Temple, in the midst of His divine attendants, holding court upon the New Year's Day and fixing the destiny of Israel for the ensuing year. It is altogether probable that the picture is based, in considerable part at least, upon a Babylonian original, for in Babylonian literature Bel-Marduk is frequently represented as discharging this function upon just this occasion.[57] Moreover, on this day the Babylonian deities, and particularly Marduk, were thought to enter their temples in solemn procession. Undoubtedly the seraphim here, just as the cherubim of Ezekiel and of postexilic literature, are largely, although probably not entirely, nor necessarily directly, an outgrowth of Babylonian representations of heavenly beings of secondary rank, the attendants of the gods.[58]

But Is. 6 does not necessarily conceive of Yahwe as actually dwelling within the Temple, and therefore constantly enthroned upon the high seat upon which the prophet beheld Him. Rather in all likelihood, very much like Marduk in the Babylonian New Year's Day ceremonial,[59] He was conceived of in the time of Isaiah as coming into the Temple only on this one day and only for the purpose of there holding His

[56a] Cf. Amos 3. 7.
[57] Cf. Zimmern, *Die Keilinschriften und das Alte Testament*[3], 515; Jastrow, *Die Religion Babyloniens und Assyriens*, I, 503.
[58] Cf. note 71, below.
[59] Cf. Zimmern, *Das babylonische Neujahrsfest*; Langdon, *The Babylonian Epic of Creation*.

divine court and pronouncing the destiny of Israel for the year. It is indeed significant that this passage calls the Temple only by the colorless name, הֵיכָל, a name which also came to Israel from the Babylonians, and that apparently it is not called by the more specific name, בֵּית יהוה, "house" or "dwelling-place of Yahwe," in a single authenticated passage earlier than Jeremiah.[60]

In other words, this narrative establishes no more than that Isaiah does see Yahwe enthroned in the Temple at Jerusalem, and this apparently upon the New Year's Day. But this evidence alone is insufficient to determine whether Yahwe was actually regarded by the prophet as residing permanently in the Temple, or as merely having entered there, of course in the form of the *kebod Yahwe*, for just that one day, in order to there hold His divine court and fix the destinies of Israel, and perhaps of other nations also, for the new year.

---

[60] Unless perhaps in Mic. 3. 12. But there הבית, in the term הר הבית, might refer to the royal palace as well as to the Temple. Moreover, of all the eighteen passages in Jeremiah in which the term בית יהוה is used, not a single one comes from the period of his prophetic activity preceding the Deuteronomic reformation in 621 B. C. The term is used very rarely in pre-Jeremian writings, and never refers specifically to the Temple at Jerusalem. Scholars are agreed that the term בית יהוה in Hos. 8. 1, and probably also in 9. 15, refers to the entire land of Palestine. And in Hos. 9. 4 the expression refers to any sanctuary of Yahwe, and particularly to the Yahwe-sanctuaries of the Northern Kingdom. In II Sam. 12. 20, clause αγ, in which the term occurs, is manifestly a late, disturbing gloss. In Josh. 6. 24 the term is likewise recognized by all scholars as an anachronism and therefore a gloss. I have shown too ("The Oldest Document, &c.," *HUCA*, IV [1927], 50) that Ex. 23. 19 and 34. 36, in which the term occurs, are both Deuteronomic. In Jud. 19. 18 the expression is also, in the opinion of all scholars, the result either of incorrect copying or of glossation. Is. 2. 2, 3, 5; 37. 1; 38. 20, 22; Mic. 4. 1 are all generally recognized as late. This leaves I Sam. 1. 24; 3. 15 as the only passages of the entire Bible earlier than Jeremiah in which the expression בית יהוה may be authentic. But even here, just as in Hos. 9. 4, it refers, not to the Temple at Jerusalem, but to the sanctuary at Shiloh, likewise in the Northern Kingdom. And inasmuch as 1. 9 and 3. 3 call this same sanctuary, הֵיכָל, the temptation is strong to regard this as the older term, in common use in the pre-Deuteronomic period. Just this is the term employed in Is. 6. 1 to designate the Temple at Jerusalem. Finally, Jer. 7. 4 seems to imply very positively that still in the days of the prophet the popular designation for the Temple at Jerusalem was היכל יהוה, as in Is. 6. 1, and not בית יהוה.

Certainly a century later, by the time of Jeremiah, the popular belief was that Yahwe dwelt permanently in the Temple. This is indicated not only, as has been intimated, by the designation of the Temple as בית יהוה, "the house of Yahwe," which becomes common from that time on, but also by the emphatic manner in which Deuteronomic writers represent the Temple at Jerusalem as the place which Yahwe had chosen, לשכן שמו שם, "to cause His name to dwell there."

But it is equally certain that this emphatic representation of the Temple as the place where Yahwe's name, i.e. of course, Yahwe Himself, dwells is with these Deuteronomic writers, in part at least, propagandistic, conforming to and enforcing the Deuteronomic program of the destruction of the local shrines throughout the country, with the Jerusalem Temple alone left as the sole place of Yahwe worship, the only place where He might be found. In fact it is difficult to believe that, so long as many sanctuaries existed in the land, all of them, regardless of possible Canaanite origins, looked upon popularly as Yahwe shrines and seats of Yahwe worship, the Temple at Jerusalem should have been generally regarded as the sole, actual abode of Yahwe, the one place where He was thought to dwell permanently. Such a concept could logically have developed only after and as a direct outgrowth of the Deuteronomic program of the destruction of all local sanctuaries other than the Temple at Jerusalem. But with only one sanctuary consecrated to Him, what more natural than that Yahwe should have speedily come to be regarded as actually dwelling permanently in that one sanctuary, in its innermost recesses? This argument is substantiated by the fact which we have already noted, that apparently not until Jeremiah, i.e. not until the Deuteronomic period, does the term בית יהוה, "house of Yahwe," become the regular designation for the Temple at Jerusalem.

This conclusion is borne out also by other considerations, secondary in character, it is true, yet of considerable significance in this connection. Ezekiel, too, unquestionably conceived of Yahwe as dwelling permanently within the Temple, for, in 10. 19 ff. and 11. 22 f. he sees the Deity, in the form of the k^ebod 'elohe Yisra'el, leaving the Temple, now doomed to destruction, going out through the eastern gate and journeying eastward over the Mount of Olives. Obviously Ezekiel could not have pictured Yahwe leaving the Temple in this manner, if he had not conceived of Him as actually dwelling there permanently. This conclusion is confirmed, as has already been intimated, by the sequel to this picture in chapters 40 ff. where the prophet gives in detail his vision of the rebuilt Temple and of the return therein of the Deity, still in the form of the k^ebod 'elohe Yisra'el, entering through the same eastern gate through which He had departed from the old Temple. The vision then concludes with the charge that this eastern gate must be kept closed forever, not only, manifestly, that no mortal being may thereafter presume to enter by the same gate as that through which the Deity had entered, but also, as we have already suggested, because, so the prophet means to imply, having taken up His permanent abode there, Yahwe will never again forsake His Temple, will never again have occasion to go out through this eastern gate. And dwelling permanently there, the Temple has now become the place of Yahwe's throne and of the resting-place of the soles of His feet.[61]

But it is quite certain that even to Ezekiel there is something of novelty about this conception of Yahwe dwelling permanently in the Temple and never again coming in or going out through the eastern gate. For, on the one hand, the prophet is compelled to legislate about the matter, and to prescribe that the eastern gate must henceforth be kept closed forever, i. e. it must never again be opened, in accordance with past custom, upon the two equinoctial days. As has been suggested, through this prescription the prophet aimed to terminate completely an old, important and long practiced ceremony, that of greeting the first rays of the rising sun upon the equinoctial days, and particularly upon the New Year's Day, a ceremony which He recognized as distinctly non-Yahwistic, and which he regarded as particularly abhorrent to Yahwe. And, on the other hand, as 8. 16 shows,

[61] Ezek. 43. 7.

this ceremony was actually practiced in the Temple at Jerusalem down to the actual moment of its destruction in 586 B.C. But with this ceremony, representing the coming of Yahwe into the Temple with the first rays of the rising sun upon each recurring New Year's Day, persisting to this late date, it is difficult to believe that the conception of Yahwe dwelling permanently in the Temple had as yet taken firm root in the belief of the people by the time of the destruction of the Temple. It would seem rather that during the century or century and a half preceding the destruction of the Temple two partially contradictory ideas were struggling for dominance in the popular belief, the old idea of the annual entrance of Yahwe into the Temple, in the form of the k^ebod Yahwe, the first rays of the rising sun, upon the New Year's Day, and the new conception, apparently supported by the prophetic group and the Deuteronomic writers, and strongly enforced by the Deuteronomic reformation and the destruction of the local sanctuaries, that the Temple at Jerusalem was the actual abode of Yahwe, His house or home, where He sat permanently enthroned in the midst of Israel.

The struggle between these two contradictory concepts continued down to the very destruction of the Temple in 586 B.C., however with the younger concept of the Temple as the permanent dwelling-place of Yahwe apparently gaining ground steadily, even though slowly. It was Ezekiel who finally decided the conflict by denouncing the old ceremony as non-Yahwistic, and by legislating that henceforth the eastern gate might never again be opened. Thereby he put an end in a very practical manner to the observance of the old sun-rite. Actually therefore it was not until the second Temple and the post-exilic period that the new concept of the Temple as the sole and permanent residence of Yahwe came to hold undisputed sway.[62] Haggai and Zechariah were

---

[62] However, even in post-Biblical times certain survivals of the old ceremony of the opening and closing of the eastern gate of the Temple, and other rites attendant upon the coming of the k^ebod Yahwe upon the New Year's Day, continued in folk-practice, and even in official religion. I have already pointed out the rôle which the closed eastern gate played in the

apparently the first therefore who, without being troubled by any contradictory and competing idea, could unqualifiedly represent the Temple at Jerusalem as the dwelling-place of ceremonies of the *simḥat bet haso'ebah* during the Succoth-festival (Sukkah, V, 4). During the Latin Kingdom in Jerusalem (1099-1187 A.D.) on two annual festivals, Palm Sunday and the Festival of the Cross, the eastern gate of the Temple area, the so-called Golden Gate, which had been sealed up during the period of Moslem possession of the city (637-1099), was opened at dawn and closed again at sunset, to remain closed during the entire remainder of the year (on the evidence of John of Würzburg, who visited Jerusalem in 1137). These two festivals are late, Christianized forms of the earlier Canaanite and Israelite equinoctial festivals, and are celebrated still today almost at the exact time of the two equinoxes (cf. my " The Three Calendars of Ancient Israel," *HUCA*, I [1924], 48 f., note 47).

In the Jewish liturgy the closing portion of the ritual for Yom Kippur is known as *Neilah*, " closing," or in its full form, *N^e'ilat Haša'ar*, " the closing of the gate," and the liturgy for this service contains frequent reference to the closing of the gate at sunset. The origin of this peculiar symbolism has never been adequately determined. But when we remember that not until near the very end of the Biblical period was the institution of the Day of Atonement established (*ibid.*, 22-43), and that until this time the 10th day of the seventh month had been steadily observed as the New Year's Day, the day therefore upon which the eastern gate of the Temple was opened at dawn and closed at sunset, it is clear that the *Neilah*-service of Yom Kippur rests upon a distinct reminiscence of the old, idolatrous rite celebrated upon this day.

Quite obviously too Ps. 24. 7-10 with its apostrophe to the gates to lift themselves up, i.e. of course, to open, so that Yahwe, the " King of Glory," or perhaps better in the light of this study, " the radiant King," i.e. Yahwe coming in the form of the *k^{e}bod Yahwe*, might enter, finds its explanation in the ceremony of opening the eastern gate of the Temple on the New Year's Day. Quite significantly both LXX and Vulg. have the introductory record, missing in M.T., that this psalm was for Sunday, while Pesh. has the fuller statement, that it was for the first day, i.e. Sunday, when God finished the work of creation. Certainly this last is an elaboration of the original statement of LXX and Vulg. And why this particular psalm should have been designated as for Sunday, and likewise why reference to this fact should be omitted in M.T., is clear when we remember that in the pre-Pharisean form of the Jewish calendar the New Year's Day, as well as all other significant festival days, fell upon Sunday. (Cf. my " The Origin of Maṣṣoth and the Maṣṣoth-Festival," *AJT*, XXI [1917], 279, and my " Additional Notes on 'The Three Calendars of Ancient Israel,' " *HUCA*, III [1926], 87-100.) This entire subject of the solar ceremonies connected with the eastern gate of the Temple at Jerusalem is obviously or far-reaching importance for the history of Judaism and of Christianity also. But it is likewise of such complexity and magnitude that it will require independent treatment. This study I shall publish at the earliest opportunity.

Yahwe to which He was about to return, still in the form of the *kebod Yahwe*,[63] in order to take up His permanent residence there in Israel's midst. Therefore Haggai could compare the Temple as Yahwe's residence with the houses in which the people themselves dwelt.[64] And Zechariah could represent Yahwe as returning to Jerusalem, to His house, and dwelling there in Israel's midst, where eventually all the nations of the earth would seek and find Him.[65]

This argument, with its important conclusions, is borne out by one further, significant piece of evidence. If, in accordance with the old belief, Yahwe was thought to come into the Temple on the morning of each recurring New Year's Day, the question arises, how was He conceived as coming; how was He transported thither? The presence in the Temple of the horses and chariots of the sun, destroyed by Josiah at the very beginning of the Deuteronomic reformation,[66] suggests the answer. Certainly these horses and chariots of the sun were present in Yahwe's Temple for no vain purpose nor as mere monuments of the cult of some foreign deity accorded a measure of worship by Israel during this period. These chariots and horses of the sun sprang unquestionably from the cult of some foreign deity, perhaps the Babylonian Shamash or else, and perhaps more probably, some West-Semitic form of the sun-god. But they must have been integrated with the worship of Yahwe in the Temple at Jeru-

[63] Cf. Hag. 1. 8 and my "On Leviticus 10. 3" in *Oriental Studies Dedicated to Paul Haupt*, 101, note 5.   [64] 1. 4, 9.

[65] 1. 16; 8. 3, 21 ff. Moreover Zechariah apparently conceived of Yahwe as dwelling, during the period between 586 and 516 B.C., during which time the Temple lay in ruins, in a place far to the east (to be inferred from the fact that the chariots coming out from the presence of Yahwe [Zech. 6. 5] go towards the north, the west [reading for אל־אחריהם, אל־האחרון, or perhaps, by analogy with the parallel expressions, אל ארץ האחרון] and the south), behind the two copper mountains. Manifestly this is the place of sunrise. The picture is clearly based upon a Babylonian original, for in Babylonian art the representation of Shamash, the sun-god, coming forth from between two mountains, is extremely common (cf. Ward, *The Seal Cylinders of Western Asia*, 87 ff. [illustrations 244–269]; Jastrow, *Bildermappe zur Religion Babyloniens und Assyriens*, 170, 171). These two mountains depicted upon these Babylonian seals were probably conceived of as copper, since burnished copper is universally symbolic of the sun, because of its color and reflective qualities.   [66] II Ki. 23. 11.

salem in such manner that they had come to seem a quite essential part of His cult. Now what functions could they have discharged, or what could their symbolism have been in the syncretistic Yahwe-cult in the Temple in that day? There can be little doubt that Yahwe was thought to come from the east and to enter the Temple riding in His chariot, the chariot of the sun, drawn by the horses of the sun. This picture probably suggested to Ezekiel his very confused and obscure conception of the manner in which the *kebod Yahwe* was carried along, both when it withdrew from the old, doomed Temple and when it approached to enter the new Temple. It would be fruitless to attempt to analyze Ezekiel's picture in detail. It suffices to remember that rabbinic tradition conceived of it as a chariot, or rather as *the* chariot, i. e. of course, the chariot of Yahwe.[67] And in fact pre-rabbinic, late Biblical tradition identified the cherubim of the ark of the Priestly Code and of later Biblical writings with this chariot, which, it was believed, had stood in the Temple from the day of its erection by Solomon.[68] Moreover, since Ezekiel speaks of the four wheels,[69] associated with the four chariots, the chariot or chariots of the sun in the Temple at Jerusalem were probably of the four-wheeled kind.[70] Mani-

[67] Cf. Torczyner, "Die Bundeslade und die Anfänge der Religion Israels," *Festschrift zum 50jährigen Bestehen der Hochschule für die Wissenschaft des Judentums*, 227 ff.   [68] I Chron. 28. 18.   [69] 1. 15–21; 10. 9–17.
[70] Cf. the illustrations in Ward, *op. cit*, nos. 976–979 (pp. 310 ff.). According to Ward these seal-cylinders are all of Syro-Hittite origin, and with the Syrian or Phoenician element outweighing the Hittite. This fact may well point to some Phoenician, or at least general West-Semitic elements in this worship of Yahwe with the attributes of a solar deity in the Temple at Jerusalem, and especially in this particular detail of the manifestly composite picture of Ezekiel. Significantly enough in no Babylonian seal inscription, so far as I have been able to discover, is the sun-god depicted riding in a chariot. The customary symbol of the sun-god travelling across the heavens is the winged disc of the sun (cf. Ward, *op. cit*, illustrations 670, 673, 678, 679, 682, 684, 685, 687, 692, 695, 714, 718; Jastrow, *op. cit*, 49, 50, 51, 56, 216, 217). It is, of course, this Babylonian representation of the winged disc of the sun to which Mal. 3. 20 refers, "Unto you who fear My name, the sun of righteousness shall arise with healing on its wings." (Recent discoveries made in the excavations at Ur and in Drak tend to disprove the above conclusion that four-wheeled chariots were known only to the Western Semites.)

festly therefore, even though Ezekiel conceived of Yahwe as dwelling permanently in the Temple at Jerusalem, and endeavored strenuously to strengthen this concept in the popular imagination and doctrine, and at the same time to root out the old belief in the coming into the Temple of Yahwe, invested with the attributes of a solar deity, in His chariot on the morning of each recurring New Year's Day, nevertheless he could not free even himself entirely from the old symbolism. When compelled to describe the departure of Yahwe from the old Temple, and later His return to the new Temple, he had no alternative but to have recourse to the traditional, popular conception of Yahwe transported in a chariot. But at the same time, though probably inadvertently, he confused his picture not a little by the introduction of various additional, but ofttimes parallel and superfluous elements, most of them seemingly, such as the figures of the cherubim, borrowed, though perhaps not altogether directly, from Babylonian pictography.[71]

[71] Cf. Jastrow, *op. cit.*, 55, 57, 63a, 63c; also 31, 32, 35, 56, 58, 59, 60, 62, 63b, 63g, 63h, 64; Ward, *op. cit.*, 42, 1149. It is noteworthy that in Jastrow, 55, 63a and 63c, and also in both illustrations cited from Ward, the figures, which we may well call cherubim, have six wings, two upper wings, that may be regarded as covering the face, two lower wings, which actually do cover the feet and the entire lower part of the body, and two wings standing out from the shoulders, manifestly designed for flying. In the other illustrations cited above, only the first and last pairs of wings are definitely represented in their regular form. The pair of wings covering the lower part of the body has been conventionalized into a decoration or fringe of the skirt hanging from the waist to the feet, but in every case having a decidedly wing-like appearance. Undoubtedly this decoration or fringe is but the conventional substitute for the older and more original third pair of wings. But these cherubim are identical with the seraphim of Is. 6. 2 in this most essential respect of the six wings. This is, in fact, the one, outstanding detail of the appearance of the seraphim which Is. 6. 2 mentions. Unquestionably the figures of the seraphim of Is. 6 were borrowed more or less directly from these Babylonian cherubim, and point to immediate Babylonian influence in the prophet's picture, and with this, of course, in his conception of the manner and purpose of Yahwe's entrance into the Temple on New Year's Day.

On the other hand, as we have already pointed out, Ezekiel's picture of the cherubim and of the $k^e bod\ Yahwe$ carried along by them, seems to be a bit more composite and to betray indications not only of Babylonian, but also of West-Semitic, and likewise of Egyptian influence. For unquestionably, as Gressmann has suggested (*Die Lade Jahves*, 50f.) the eyes in the wheels (Ezek.

This significant fact too points to the conclusion that the conception of Yahwe carried along in a chariot was still extremely lively in Ezekiel's day. But this picture of Yahwe must be linked up with the conception of Him as not yet dwelling permanently and solely in the Temple at Jerusalem, and therefore requiring a vehicle of transportation, in which He would come regularly on the morning of each recurring New Year's Day, coming from the east in the rôle of a solar deity, to exercise judgment in the midst of His heavenly host and to determine the destinies of Israel, and perhaps of other nations also, for the year just beginning.[72] Just this is the picture of Yahwe in Is. 6.

All this evidence, although secondary in character, is none the less of extreme interest and importance for the history of the religion of Israel. Above all it corroborates our previous conclusion that Isaiah did not yet definitely conceive of the Temple at Jerusalem as the actual, permanent dwelling-place of Yahwe, that this conception, although by no means unheard of before, began to gain ground steadily only with the Deuteronomic reformation at the end of the 7th century B.C., and that it did not become the dominant conception in the religious belief and practice of Israel until the early post-exilic period and the erection of the second Temple. It was Ezekiel apparently, in the latest stages of his prophetic ministry, who contributed most to the final triumph of this youngest concept of Yahwe and of His relation to the Temple at Jerusalem.

The three stages in the development of the conception of Yahwe in ancient Israel, which must be correlated with the three stages in the evolution of the conception of the ark are then, (1) the first stage, in which early, more or less primitive, local or tribal conceptions of Yahwe are gradually coalescing under the influence of evolving national life, and the con-

---

10. 12) represent an adaptation of the Horus-eye, not infrequently met with in Egyptian pictography.

[72] In the Babylonian religion Shamash, the sun-god *par excellence*, regularly plays the rôle of the divine judge (Zimmern, *Die Keilinschriften und das Alte Testament*,[3] 368; Jastrow, *Die Religion Babyloniens und Assyriens*, cf. index, II, 1098), even though it was Marduk, or, in some texts, Nebo, who fixed the destinies upon the New Year's Day (Zimmern, *op. cit.*, 515).

ception of a single, national Yahwe is slowly evolving; (2) the second stage, in which Yahwe, yielding to the syncretizing influence of agricultural environment and culture and its related Baal-worship, and perhaps also to growing Assyro-Babylonian cultural influence, is endowed with various attributes of a solar deity and, associated particularly intimately with the national sanctuary, the Temple at Jerusalem, is conceived of as coming there on each recurrent New Year's Day to administer justice and to fix the destinies of Israel, and with it, in all likelihood, the destinies of all other nations with which Israel had relations;[73] (3) the third stage, beginning with the Deuteronomic reformation, when, as the result of prophetic attempts at purification of the religion of Israel of all non-Yahwistic elements, Yahwe is, at least outwardly and superficially, divested of the most obvious and objectionable attributes of a solar deity, and comes now to be regarded as dwelling permanently and solely in the Temple at Jerusalem, enthroned in its innermost recesses, in the midst of His people Israel.

With these three stages in the evolution of the conception of Yahwe in ancient Israel the three stages in the evolution of the conception of the ark and its functions, which we have

[73] The thought suggests itself that the conception of the Day of Yahwe sprang, in part at least, out of this celebration of the entrance of Yahwe, in the form of the radiant $k^ebod\ Yahwe$, into the Temple at Jerusalem on the New Year's Day in order to hold His divine court and to fix the destinies of Israel and the other nations. The earliest picture of the Day of Yahwe which we have, and in many respects also the most vivid, is that of Amos 5. 18 ff. The context there is rather loose and not a little bit obscure. But assuming the unity of the passage, which is, however, not absolutely certain, the popular belief of the time of Amos seems to have been that the Day of Yahwe was to be a day of festival (so also Sellin, *Das Zwölfprophetenbuch*, vol. XII of his *Kommentar zum Alten Testament* series, 193), a day of sacrifice (so also Zeph. 1. 7 f.) and merry-making, and apparently of carrying the images or symbols of the gods in solemn procession, presumably into the Temple. It was also a day of light and radiance, such as would naturally be associated with the coming of the $k^ebod\ Yahwe$. Above all else it was the day of Yahwe's judgment upon and fixing the destinies of Israel and of all nations (vv. 19 and 24; cf. also Is. 2. 4; Mi. 4. 3; Zeph. 3. 8; Joel 4. 1 ff.). All these elements in this conception of the Day of Yahwe find their most simple and natural explanation in the assumption of outgrowth out of the celebration of Yahwe's entrance in the form of the $k^ebod\ Yahwe$ into the Temple upon the New Year's Day.

noted, go hand in hand. In the first stage Yahwe was conceived of primarily as a local or tribal deity, with the conception slowly expanding and evolving into that of an intertribal, and eventually into that of a national deity. This last conception of Yahwe naturally could eventuate completely only with the actual evolution of the nation itself under David. During this stage we find the ark likewise still conceived of in its most primitive form, as a box containing something, whatever it may have been, thought to be charged with divine power. By virtue of this power, carried into battle against Israel's foes, it could give victory to its people, or in the midst of a foreign, hostile nation it could discomfit its enemies, or once more restored to its own people, it could bring blessing to the inmates of the house in which it stood, or it could select of its own accord the way it wished to go and lead its people in safety along this way through the desert until they eventually arrived at the goal which it had appointed for them.

In the second period, which, we have seen, continued down to the Deuteronomic reformation, and which was actually not completely superseded until the end of the Babylonian exile, the conception of Yahwe underwent various changes and modifications. During this entire period Israel was subjected constantly to strong foreign cultural influences. The result was a steady process of syncretization of Yahwe with various foreign deities, and of His worship with strange cults. Actually this process had begun in the preceding period in the natural fusion of the old, tribal, desert Yahwe with the many Canaanitish Baals. This process had apparently gone on quietly, steadily and largely unconsciously on the part of the people almost from the moment of Israel's settlement in Canaan and adoption of the Canaanitish agricultural life and culture. Apparently certain fundamental elements of the Canaanitish, agricultural, Baal cult, such as the three annual agricultural festivals, Matzoth, Qatsir and Asif, and also the Sabbath, had become so thoroughly integrated in the established Yahweworship already in the early period of national existence, following the reign of David, that even the most ardent champions of the supposedly old and pure Yahwe-worship failed to realize their true, non-Yahwistic origin, and so included due provision for their observance in their first systematic formulation of fundamental and approved Yahwe-worship.[74]

But with the reign of Solomon, with its strongly centralized and efficient system of government, with its developing economic prosperity, increasing commercial activity and expanding contacts and relations with foreign nations and cultures, the conception of Yahwe tended to undergo further modification and syncretization. The national sanctuary at Jerusalem, but recently erected as the central shrine of Israel's national god, became likewise, and almost immediately, the seat of the worship in Israel of various foreign deities. Naturally the cults of these deities, for the most part more developed, elaborate and complex than the still comparatively simple cult of Yahwe, influenced considerably both the worship and also the conception of Yahwe, and tended to introduce into them new, and by no means always logical, consistent and perfectly harmonizable elements and ideas. It was this condition which in large part gave rise to the prophetic group or party, whose basic principle was the championship of the traditional, even though not always actually the historically true, original and simple desert worship of Yahwe. We have seen that the first, organized and systematic attempt of this party to carry out its program was made in the Southern Kingdom in 899 B.C., with the reformation of Asa.[75] It was directed against the worship of Yahwe in the form of images or idols, fostered by the court party. Apparently it sought even to revive and substitute the old "tent of meeting" of the tribe of Judah for the Temple at Jerusalem. We have seen that this reformation succeeded only in part, that it did apparently counteract successfully the prevalent idol-worship of the day, and did likewise formulate a positive program of orthodox Yahwe-worship. But in its apparent endeavor to substitute the old "tent of meeting" for the new and elaborate Temple it failed completely.

[74] Cf. "The Oldest Document, &c.," *HUCA*, IV (1927), 63 f. and 73–79.
[75] *Ibid.*, 98–119 and 123–127.

Nor were these prophetic activities, with their steadfast opposition to foreign, non-Yahwistic cults, confined only to the Southern Kingdom, nor did they center only around the Temple at Jerusalem. A bare third of a century after the reformation of Asa in the Southern Kingdom we find Elijah waging the same contest against the worship of the Phoenician Baal in the Northern Kingdom, and his work carried on after his death by his successor, Elisha.

During this period the foreign cultural influences to which both the Northern and the Southern Kingdoms were subjected, were many and varied. The Phoenician influence apparently was the first to make itself felt. It was largely through Phoenician merchants that the commercial activities of the reigns of David and Solomon were fostered, and it was after the model of Phoenician merchant fleets in the Mediterranean that Solomon organized his commercial expeditions to the Red Sea and Indian Ocean countries.[76] The Temple at Jerusalem was erected by Phoenician architects and artisans, with materials largely brought from Phoenicia, and after the model of Phoenician temples. Small wonder that the reformers in the days of Asa looked upon it more or less askance, and doubted, or even denied, its true Yahwe-character. This Phoenician culture was apparently itself more or less composite, with native elements considerably influenced by Egyptian, Hittite and Assyro-Babylonian cultures and religious concepts and practices. The period of direct and dominant Phoenician cultural influence in Israel, in both the Northern and Southern Kingdoms extended from the reigns of David and Solomon through the reigns of the entire dynasty of Omri. It reached its climax during and after the reign of Ahab under the guidance of the strong-minded and energetic Jezebel. It was this Phoenician cultural influence which was combatted uncompromisingly and largely unsuccessfully by Elijah, and less uncompromisingly but, outwardly at least, more successfully by Elisha. The culmination of the conflict was, of course, the revolution of Elisha and Jehu, with the murder of the entire

---

[76] II Ki. 9. 26–28; 10. 22.

house of Ahab and the attendant religious reformation in 842 B.C. The outcome was a nominal, but altogether superficial, and from the political and economic standpoints disastrous, triumph for the champions of the supposedly old and pure Yahwe-worship. Actually, as was to be expected, elements of the superior Phoenician culture had penetrated too deeply into Israelite life and thought, and taken too firm root, to be easily and speedily eradicated.

At just about the time of the Elisha-Jehu revolution and reformation the contact of Israel with Assyria became immediate, and apparently the influence of Assyro-Babylonian culture direct and of steady growth. Unfortunately the period of almost a century following immediately upon this revolution has left few authentic historical records. Not until the prophetic writings near the end of this period do we begin to get a clear picture of the religious, social and economic life of the two kingdoms. Then we find that during this period the cultural life of the people of both Northern and Southern Kingdoms had undergone a very considerable change and taken a decided step forward.

Now for the first time we meet, in Is. 6, the picture of Yahwe with His *kabod*, His radiance, enthroned in the Temple at Jerusalem upon the New Year's Day, surrounded by His seraphim, angelic creatures, and holding court and deciding the destinies of Israel and the nations for the ensuing year. This is our earliest record of the concept of Yahwe in the form of the k^ebod $Yahwe$ of later Biblical writings and of the *shechina* of Rabbinic literature and theology; and seemingly in Is. 6 this concept is still somewhat incipient in character. We have seen that many and the most dominant of the elements of this picture have their precedents and parallels in Babylonian theology and literature, and that the picture as a whole, even though not necessarily in all its details, is undoubtedly dependent upon a Babylonian original. We find but few traces of any of the elements of this picture in the records of the belief and practice of earlier periods of Israelite history.[77]

---

[77] Unless perhaps in the fact that the Temple at Jerusalem, like many of its Phoenician models (as for example the great temple at Hierapolis

Unquestionably it was a concept of Yahwe which had developed during just this period and very largely under the influence of Babylonian religious belief and practice.

As has been said, this picture of Yahwe is predominantly that of a sun-god. Yahwe is here invested with the attributes and is represented as discharging certain of the functions of Babylonian solar deities, particularly Shamash and Marduk. All this had little relationship with the original, simple concept of Yahwe during the desert period of Israel's history or the early sojourn in Palestine. Yahwe had travelled a long road indeed, and undergone a far-reaching and momentous development and transformation in concept and mode of worship since that early, primitive day. Of all this the prophets must have been more or less conscious, even though apparently the great pre-exilic prophets, with Hosea as a possible partial exception, troubled themselves less about these matters apparently than they did about the to them far more significant and serious,

[Lucian, *De Dea Syra*, 29 (ed. Jacobitz, III, 355)]; cf. also Robinson, *Biblical Researches in Palestine and in the Adjacent Regions*, III, 417, 426, 437, 507 ff. [the two great temples at Baalbek]; Porter, *Five Years in Damascus*, I, 294; Blau, " Early Christian Archaeology from the Jewish Point of View," *HUCA*, III [1926], 171) faced the east. Some traces may perhaps also be found in the tradition of Elijah's bringing down fire from heaven (I Ki. 18) and in David's bringing up the ark to Jerusalem (II Sam. 6; I Chron. 16); for there is considerable evidence that both of these incidents happened in connection with the celebration of the Asif- or Succoth-festival and the New Year's Day following immediately thereupon. This matter is, however, of such extent and complexity that it must await separate treatment elsewhere. But at the very most all this would indicate only that some elements of the eventual picture of the k^ebod $Yahwe$ coming into the Temple on the New Year's Day were of Canaanite, Phoenician or West-Semitic origin, and that they had entered, as was but natural, since this was in itself a festival of Canaanite or common West-Semitic origin, into the celebration of the Asif-festival and the New Year's Day already in the days of David, Solomon and Elijah, and were not even discountenanced by the latter prophet. But this does not alter the fact that the particular picture of Yahwe, enveloped in the *kabod* and with the Temple filled with cloud or smoke, sitting as judge and arbiter of the destinies of nations, surrounded by the heavenly court, on the New Year's Day, has its most immediate and striking parallel, and unquestionably in many details also its direct antecedent, in Babylonian theology and literature, and that in this picture, composite as it obviously is, already in the days of Isaiah Babylonian elements seem to have predominated.

inward, spiritual transgressions of the true worship of Yahwe. None the less these facts and conditions must have influenced the program of the prophetic party as a group directly and considerably during this period. Unquestionably it helped to formulate the anti-foreign policy of Isaiah, and it likewise animated the reform movement in the reign of Hezekiah, which culminated in the destruction of the brazen serpent in the Temple.[78]
The eradication of solar elements in the cult of Yahwe in the Temple at Jerusalem was likewise a part of the program of the Deuteronomic reformation, as the reference in II Ki. 23. 11 to the chariots and horses of the sun indicates. And, as we have seen, it was Ezekiel, a more superficial, conventional and formal prophet, with less insight into the inward, spiritual implications of his prophetic mission, who denounced the significant ceremony of the greeting of the rising sun upon the New Year's Day uncompromisingly, and who eventually, finding it too firmly rooted in popular belief and practice to be completely eradicated, sought, and apparently with considerable success, to reinterpret the character of this rite and its underlying concepts and to legitimize it and incorporate it positively into the recognized prophetic conception of Yahwe and His worship. As has been said, the reaction of the Deuteronomic writers and of Ezekiel to the foreign, syncretizing influences

---

[78] II Ki. 18. 4. This does not mean necessarily that the brazen serpent was itself the product of this period. A very probable conjecture is that it was originally, precisely like the ark, an old, tribal cult object, which David had deposited is his national sanctuary at Jerusalem for the same reason that he brought the ark thither, to give to the members of all the tribes concrete and ocular proof that Yahwe was now truly a national, and no longer merely a tribal deity, that He was now the summation of all the old tribal gods. Thereby David sought to contribute to the popular regard for the Temple at Jerusalem as the national sanctuary and place of pilgrimage for all the tribes, and thus to strengthen the unity of his nation.

The brazen serpent in the Temple may very profitably be compared with the dove and gazelle images in the Ka'aba in the "days of ignorance" (cf. Robertson Smith, *The Religion of the Semites*,[2] 298). Likewise the presence of many idols in the Ka'aba in the period immediately preceding Mohammed, in all likelihood the images or cult-objects of various, old, tribal deities, gave to the Ka'aba the character of an intertribal sanctuary. In this it presents an interesting and significant parallel to David's sanctuary at Jerusalem and his manifest purpose

and the developing conception and representation of Yahwe as a solar deity brought to an end this second period in the evolution of the conception of Yahwe in Israel. A moment's thought makes it clear that in this rapidly developing conception and representation of Yahwe predominantly as a solar deity during this entire second period there was little room for the ark to play anything of its original rôle, or for that matter any rôle at all. And not this alone, but another important consideration enters here. Whatever may have been the actual motives of David in bringing up the ark to Jerusalem and depositing it in his tent-sanctuary, there can not be the slightest doubt that, deposited there, and subsequently in the more elaborate national sanctuary, the Temple, it necessarily came gradually to lose very much of its old significance. There is not the slightest evidence nor reason to believe that after it had been deposited in the Temple the ark was ever again taken from there and carried into battle in order to give Israel victory over its enemies. Certainly it never again had occasion or opportunity to select the way it wanted to go or to lead Israel upon a long, difficult and uncertain journey. Nor could it have long continued to be regarded as the very seat or container in the Temple of the potent, divine power associated with the being of Yahwe. In the vision of Isaiah the ark plays no rôle whatsoever, and Yahwe is seated, not upon it, but upon a high chair or throne. Nor is the ark mentioned at all, with regard to its place or rôle in the Temple during this period, in any of the writings of this time. Nor can the ark be integrated in any conceivable way with the picture which seems to have been dominant during this period, of Yahwe coming into the Temple in the form of the *k^{e}bod Yahwe*, the first rays of the

to represent this as intertribal and national in character. Furthermore, the removal of these idols from the Kaʿaba, following Mohammed's new preachment, is likewise not without significant parallelism with the reformation of Hezekiah, and even more with the Deuteronomic reformation. And the sparing of the Kaʿaba, the sacred stone itself, and the new interpretation and rôle given to it in the ritual of Islam also parallel significantly and illuminatingly the sparing of the ark in these reformations and the new interpretation given to it in the subsequent religion of Israel.

rising sun upon the New Year's Day, and there holding His divine court. And, as we have seen, in his scheme of the rebuilt Temple Ezekiel makes no provision whatsoever for the ark, quite as if it was an object of no particular consequence; in Deut. 1. 33 and 42 reference to the ark is purposely suppressed, just as if it was regarded as not altogether in accord with basic Deuteronomic principles of Yahwe-concept and worship; and Jer. 3. 16 speaks of it as having been an object of considerable religious significance in the popular belief of a former day, but of no real significance at all, and therefore entirely dispensable, in the more advanced, enlightened and true conception of Yahwe and His worship of the day of the author of this passage; in fact the implication of the verse is that the worship of Yahwe is purer and the religion of Israel truer without the ark than with it. Seemingly the authors of Deut. 1. 33 and 42 and of Jer. 3. 16 attributed to the ark much the same non-Yahwistic significance as that which the brazen serpent enjoyed at the time of the reformation of Hezekiah.

Therefore because of the syncretistic conception of Yahwe which developed so rapidly during this period, and the utter incompatibility with it of the old conception of the ark and its functions, one of two things had to happen to the ark; either it had to lose its significance as a sacred object entirely, and suffer a fate identical with that of the brazen serpent in the Temple, viz. prophetic denunciation and destruction, or it had to undergo a process of reinterpretation of far-reaching compass and significance. Actually both fates befell it in the course of time; and not only the ark, but, at an earlier period, the brazen serpent likewise. For unquestionably the tradition of the serpents in the wilderness and of the making of the brazen serpent by Moses, recorded in Num. 21. 6–9, sprang up just because of the presence of the brazen serpent in the Temple from of old, and represented an attempt, even though vain, to justify and legitimize its presence there and thereby to save it from the fate of destruction which eventually overtook it in the reign of Hezekiah.

The ark, too, underwent both experiences of original reinterpretation and eventual disappearance, even though not, so far as our records indicate, of actual and purposed destruction in some prophetic reformation. The fact that in all probability the ark survived in the Temple so much longer than did the brazen serpent, and apparently became an object only of prophetic disregard and mild disapproval rather than of actual denunciation and destruction, can be best explained by two important considerations, viz. that it underwent a more plausible and positive reinterpretation than the brazen serpent possibly could, and also that it contained no actual image or idol, such as the brazen serpent or the *mifleṣet* of Maachah were, to which prophetic principles and program could take direct and serious exception. This last consideration offers a potent argument that, whatever the ark may have contained, it was certainly not an image of any kind.[79]

Now what was this process of reinterpretation of the character and functions of the ark during this second period of the evolution of the conception of Yahwe? It came to be regarded as the depository of the traditional two tablets of stone upon which the Ten Commandments were written. We have also seen that this process of reinterpretation seemingly began fairly early in this period, with the composition of the Book of the Covenant. But it is equally clear that this process of reinterpretation must have been rather slow and gradual and could not have taken final shape until the tradition of the Ten Commandments written upon the two stone tablets had definitely evolved. We have seen [80] that it is not at all certain whether the original Kenite Code contained ten or eight laws or "words." But certainly the nucleus of the Book of the Covenant consisted of ten "words," no more and no less.[81] But, as Ex. 24. 7 states explicitly, the Book of the Covenant represented these as written, not upon two stone tablets, but upon a scroll, in the customary manner of writing. Just when and how this last form of the tradition, viz. that of the two stone tablets, developed and what its probable antecedents may have been, we shall endeavor to determine later.

[79] Contrary to the insistent, but altogether unproved argument of Gressmann, *Die Lade Jahves*, 21 ff.
[80] "The Oldest Document, &c.," *HUCA*, IV (1927), 95 ff.
[81] *Ibid.*, 92–95.

It is apparent too that during this entire period, and even long thereafter, the ark continued to be regarded as the proper place for the deposit of various sacred objects for permanent safe-keeping and for witnessing to the power of Yahwe and to His peculiar solicitude for Israel. But under the influence of the tradition in its final form, that the ark was the depository of the two stone tablets of the Ten Commandments, and that these were objects of incomparable and inviolate sanctity, the principle seems to have evolved that other objects, no matter how sacred their character, might no longer be deposited in, but only alongside of the ark. Therefore Deut. 31. 26 commands that a copy of the Deuteronomic Torah, inscribed upon a scroll, be deposited beside the ark, and Ex. 16. 33 f. and Num. 17. 25, parts of secondary strata of the Priestly Code, make the same provision for the vessel of manna and Aaron's rod.

And with the ark now popularly regarded as containing the Book of the Covenant, or, in the final form of the tradition, the two stone tablets of the Ten Commandments, it acquired a new and positive significance, entirely unrelated to its original character and function, and with a valid and even dignified place in the prophetic tradition and program. For the prophetic tradition was that Yahwe had not always been Israel's god, but had become so only through adoption, through a covenant entered into between Him and Israel in the desert, after He had delivered Israel from Egypt. As we have seen,[82] whatever Yahwe's relations to the various tribes of Israel may have been originally, it was primarily the Yahwe of the tribe of Judah who, due to the dominant rôle which this tribe played under the leadership of David in the final establishment of the nation, and which it continued to play thereafter, particularly during the momentous reigns of David and Solomon, that the Yahwe of Judah came to contribute the most essential features to the conception of Yahwe as Israel's god. And, as we have also seen, it was Judah, with the closely associated tribes of Simon and Levi, which had come out of Egypt under the leadership of Moses, and

---

[82] *Ibid.*, 135 ff.

at the mountain in the desert had entered into covenant with Yahwe. And not this alone, but as we have also seen, Yahwe had been originally the god of the Kenites, and this tribe or clan had attached itself to the southern group of tribes, and continued until the days of Jeremiah to so live and worship that still even then they were regarded as the true devotees of Yahwe and of His proper worship. It was therefore from Judah, and with a Kenite background, that the idea of the covenant as the basis of the relationship between Yahwe and Israel had entered into prophetic tradition and come to play so important a rôle in the prophetic program.

And as the depository of the scroll, or in the final form of the tradition, the two stone tablets, upon which the laws basic to the covenant, themselves of prophetic origin, were inscribed, the ark naturally became in the eyes of the people of the Northern Kingdom, and even of active and leading spirits in the prophetic party, the symbol of the covenant, the constant reminder of the origin and nature of Yahwe's relations with Israel. As such it served a definite and positive purpose, discharged a distinct, even though a passive function; it was the eternal, ever-present, insistent witness unto Israel of Yahwe's covenant with it. This justified its presence in the Temple, even in the very holy of holies, where tradition, if not actual historic fact, placed it; and this rôle, altogether positive in its relation to Yahwe, and in no way smacking of idolatrous association, undoubtedly saved the ark during this period from the fate of the brazen serpent. It was now no longer merely the ארון יהוה, "the ark of Yahwe"; it had now become truly the ארון ברית יהוה, "the ark of the covenant of Yahwe."[83] But as the "ark of the covenant of

---

[83] We find in the Bible three general names for the ark. As is to be expected, they correspond to the three stages in the evolution of the conception of the ark and its functions. In the oldest literary strata of the Bible the ark is regularly designated as ארון יהוה (I Sam. 4. 6; 5. 3, 4; 6. 1 ff.; II Sam. 6. 9 ff.) or ארון האלהים (I Sam. 4. 4 ff.; 5. 2; 14. 18; II Sam. 6. 2 ff.; 15. 24, 25, 29), or occasionally ארון אלהי ישראל (I Sam. 5. 7, 8, 10, 11). Not infrequently in these same passages the fuller and later terms ארון ברית יהוה or ארון הברית are met with, but there is in every case good reason to believe that ברית is here a later insertion (cf. Smith, *Samuel*, in *International Critical Commentary* 33,) and not original. It

Yahwe", it had, of course, lost every trace of its original character as a source of active, divine power, as the container is clear too that the editors who inserted this term did so in order to make the name of the ark everywhere conform to the later official designation current in their day and conforming to their theology. But it is equally clear that they were not entirely consistent and thorough in this editorial process. When we come, however, to the writings of the Deuteronomic period we find this later designation of the ark used with great frequency and consistency (Deut. 10. 8; 31. 9, 25, 26; Josh. 3 *passim*; 4. 18; 7. 6; 8. 33; Jud. 20. 27b; I Ki. 3. 15; 6. 19; 8. 1 ff.; Jer. 3. 16). Furthermore, we find occasionally in writings of the post-exilic period or in insertions into passages of the older literature, where the term is again manifestly the result of editorial, theological redaction, a third and fuller designation of the ark, although with some variations, ארון ברית יהוה צבאות ישב הכרובים (I Sam. 4. 4; II Sam. 6. 2; I Chron. 13. 6).

It is self-evident that this last designation of the ark could not have developed until the picture had been clearly formulated of Yahwe enthroned in the Temple, above or between the cherubim. But, as we have seen, it was Ezekiel apparently, who first developed this picture. It is true that the seraphim of Is. 6 offered him stimulating antecedents; but these seraphim of Is. 6 are apparently not the bearers nor protectors of the throne of Yahwe, as in Ezekiel's and subsequent pictures, but are rather His attendants and the members of His heavenly court. Outside of Ezekiel the oldest Biblical reference to the cherubim is found in Gen. 3. 24; but even that passage is undoubtedly post-exilic, as the manifest dependence of the doctrine of universalism expressed in the J portions of Gen. 1–11 upon the doctrine of universalism of Deutero-Isaiah, together with other evidence, indicates. There is consequently in the entire Bible not a single, assured pre-Ezekelian, and therefore pre-exilic, reference to cherubim, and least of all to cherubim in association with the ark or the throne of Yahwe in the Temple. This is convincing evidence that the name ארון ברית יהוה צבאות ישב הכרובים is late, and the product of the third period of evolution of the conception of the ark and its functions, when it had come to be regarded primarily as the base of the *kapporet* and Yahwe's seat upon this (refuting Dibelius, *Die Lade Jahves*, 72 ff.; Gressmann, *Die Lade Jahves*, 6 ff.; Torczyner, "Die Bundeslade und die Anfänge der Religion Israels," *Festschrift zum 50 jährigen Bestehen der Hochschule für die Wissenschaft des Judentums,* 239 ff.).

Quite similarly the name ארון הברית is descriptive of the function which the ark was thought to discharge, as we have seen, in the second period of its evolution, as the receptacle of the two tablets of stone upon which, according to the tradition, the Decalogue, the basis of Yahwe's covenant with Israel, was inscribed. (For ברית = the tablets of the Decalogue cf. I Ki. 8. 21.) As the depository of these monuments of and witnesses to this covenant it was naturally designated as "the ark of the covenant of Yahwe." And this designation served an additional and significant purpose; for it tended to refute the old, and now outgrown and rejected, semi-idolatrous idea that the ark was in itself a deity, or else the container of a deity, and to emphasize the new and, at least at first,

of that which was regarded originally either as Yahwe Himself or as that in which Yahwe resided and from which the divine force, which betokened the presence of Yahwe, emanated. As the "ark of the covenant" it was no longer directly associated with the presence of Yahwe, nor did it symbolize this in any way. For, on the one hand, to symbolize the actual presence or being of Yahwe by any image or concrete object, even the ark, would undoubtedly have violated a fundamental prophetic principle. And on the other hand, as we have seen, during this second period Yahwe was apparently not yet definitely looked upon as dwelling solely and permanently in the Temple at Jerusalem, but only as coming there once a year, upon the New Year's Day.

B

THE THIRD PERIOD

In the third period, as we have seen, the conception of Yahwe became radically different. Beginning with the Deuteronomic reformation and the centralization of worship in the one, single sanctuary, the Temple at Jerusalem, gather-

rather controversial idea that the ark contained only these sacred stones and naught else, and was therefore the constant, visible symbol of Yahwe's covenant with Israel.

Finally, what seems to have been the very youngest Biblical designation of the ark, and which is found only in Priestly writings, ארון העדות (cf. above, note 41). It represents a continuation of the conception of the ark current in the second period, as the depository of the two tablets of the Decalogue, the testimony of Yahwe's covenant with Israel. But, as we have seen, the dominant Priestly conception of the ark was as the throne of Yahwe, upon which He sits eternally in the midst of His people Israel. But, as we have seen also, the secondary Priestly conception of the ark, as containing the Decalogue, therefore the "ark of testimony," was purely conventional, and without the slightest reality. Moreover, there is good reason to believe that very late Priestly writers misinterpreted, though whether consciously or not it is impossible to say, the import of the term ארון העדות. For in Ex. 30. 6, 36; Num. 17. 19 העדות, i. e. the ark, is spoken of as the place שמה (לך) אשר אועד לכם, "the place where I shall meet with you." The implication of these three passages is that the ark was called העדות or ארון העדות because it was the place where Yahwe met (אועד) with Israel. That this is, of course, a false etymology does not alter the manifest fact that these late Priestly writers, for all three verses come from secondary strata of the Priestly Code, offered this interpretation of the term העדות in all seriousness. This implies probably that to them the ark had ceased to be regarded as the depository of the two tablets of the Decalogue, and was looked upon solely as the throne of Yahwe.

ing force with Ezekiel and his vision of the rebuilt Temple, and finding its complete expression in post-exilic literature, the belief became dominant that Yahwe had taken up His permanent residence in the Temple, in the midst of Israel.[84] But dwelling now in a particular place, the limits of which were exactly defined, it was inevitable that the figure of Yahwe be concretized a bit, be given just enough of form and being and tangibility to be actually localized in this spot. This process was not difficult, even though in principle it was not altogether in conformity with prophetic doctrine. Ezekiel had paved the way for it with his picture of the *kebod Yahwe* and by prescribing that the eastern gate of the Temple must be kept tightly closed forever, thereby terminating more or less effectually the old, solar, non-Yahwistic rite of the entrance into the Temple of the first rays of the rising sun upon the New Year's Day. Thereby he symbolized, as has been said, the permanent presence of Yahwe in the Temple in the form of the *kebod Yahwe*. This doctrine gained firm hold upon the imagination of the people, and, as we have seen, even found its place in the announcements of the early post-exilic prophets, Haggai and Zechariah, that when the new Temple should have been completed, as the crowning act of the dedication ceremonies upon the New Year's Day, Yahwe would come in the form of the *kebod Yahwe*, and take up His permanent abode in the new Temple.[85] From this

---

[84] Utterances like that of Is. 66. 1, that the heavens are Yahwe's throne and the earth His footstool (cf. also I Ki. 8. 27), manifestly protesting emphatically against the idea that Yahwe should be thought to dwell or to be contained in a Temple, and at the same time reaffirming the doctrine of the absolute universality of Yahwe, His utter incorporeality and the impropriety of attempting to represent Him as confined to one particular abode, serve but to emphasize the generality of the concept of Yahwe actually dwelling in the Temple throughout the postexilic period.

[85] Hag. 1. 8; Zech. 2. 9. It is also implied in the vision of the trial of Joshua before Yahwe, holding court in the Temple and attended by angels, in Zech. 3, and in the symbolism of the golden candelabrum, in Zech. 4. This matter, however, is complex, and is obviously related to other matters already referred to, which must be reserved for treatment elsewhere. This doctrine of the coming of the *kebod Yahwe* into the Temple on the New Year's Day has likewise been introduced into the account of the dedication of Solomon's Temple, in I Ki. 8. 1–11. This was done by Priestly writers and in quite skillful manner (cf. my " The Three

time on the k^{e}bod Yahwe was thought to abide steadily in the Temple. But as yet there was not the slightest implication of the association of the k^{e}bod Yahwe in the Temple with the ark.[86] In fact we do not meet this association of the ark with the k^{e}bod Yahwe until the Priestly Code, and, as has been said, not even in the earliest portions of this, the Holiness and Torah sections of P, but only in the later Grundschrift and strata secondary to that.

But in the Grundschrift of the Priestly Code and other writings dependent thereon, Yahwe is regularly represented as sitting enthroned upon the *kapporet* between the cherubim above the ark. At the same time the ark is still the depository of the two stone tablets of the Ten Commandments, now called לחת העדות, "the tablets of testimony." Accordingly the ark is likewise designated now as the ארון העדות, "the ark of testimony." Manifestly the association of the term עדות with the ark is secondary to its association with the tablets. They are the primary testimony, and the ark is called the "ark of testimony" only because the tablets are, according to tradition, deposited in it. Consequently it is clear that the testimony of the tablets is still much the same as what it was during the second period of the evolution of the conception of Yahwe and of the ark, testimony, through the "words"

Calendars of Ancient Israel," *HUCA*, I [1924], 46). In addition to the passages cited there, careful analysis establishes with fair certainty that vv. 6b–11 of this chapter are likewise secondary and altogether Priestly in character. Without these insertions the passage is quite complete, and narrates in simple, concise form the manner in which Solomon and the elders of Israel brought up the ark from where it had been deposited by David, and reverently set it up in the innermost part of the new Temple. But it is only these inserted verses and verse fragments which introduce the picture of the k^{e}bod Yahwe, with all the attendant circumstances of the cloud filling the Temple and the priests unable to remain therein because of the cloud and the presence of the k^{e}bod Yahwe therein. Nothing of this stood in the original account of the dedication of the Temple.

[86] In fact there is good reason for believing that the ark did not yet enter into Zechariah's conception of the Temple and its equipment, and that he regarded the golden candelabrum, referred to in chap. 4, as the symbol of the presence not of the ark but of Yahwe in the Temple. This matter, too, is, however, quite complex, and related to the matters referred to above, reserved for detailed treatment elsewhere.

inscribed upon them, of the covenant which Yahwe had established with Israel when He brought them out of Egypt. But as we have already shown,[87] unquestionably this idea is only conventional and practically meaningless in P. For on the one hand, as has been said, unless they were exhibited upon occasion, or at least were capable of being exhibited, and this the presence of the golden *kapporet* upon the ark probably made impossible, the tablets could not really serve as testimony. And on the other hand, the assurance that Yahwe had taken up permanent residence in Israel's midst, and would never depart therefrom, an assurance which obviously accords completely with and sprang out of Jeremiah's message of Yahwe's new, eternal covenant with a purified, regenerated Israel, which dominated unceasingly the belief, hope and speculation of post-exilic Judaism, worked a significant change in the symbolism of the ark. It caused the old idea of the covenant relation existing between Yahwe and Israel, particularly a covenant relation which, as the earlier prophets had proclaimed repeatedly, could and would be abrogated if Israel did not keep faith with Yahwe, to lose much, in fact almost all, of its original force. Consequently there was now little or no need, as there had been in the second period, of a testimony, a constant reminder to the people of their covenant relation with Yahwe. For, on the one hand, with Yahwe now dwelling in their midst they needed no reminder of Him and His covenant; and, on the other hand, they now believed firmly that this covenant must endure forever, even though they themselves might be somewhat remiss in fulfilling the obligations it laid upon them. These considerations too make it quite clear that the entire conception of the "tablets of testimony" and of the "ark of testimony" in P was altogether conventional, had little or no positive significance, and was eventually, as we have shown, either forgotten or else purposely disregarded by late Priestly writers.

Moreover, the extreme anti-anthropomorphism of the Priestly writers caused them considerable embarrassment in this connection. On the one hand, they borrowed the figure

---

[87] Above, note 41.

of the *kebod Yahwe* from Ezekiel, but refused to represent it, as Ezekiel had done, in human shape. Instead, in accordance with their theological principles, they sought to reduce the anthropomorphism and heighten the spirituality of the conception as much as possible by representing the *kebod Yahwe* as a fiery apparition, " something like the appearance of fire," [88] enveloped in " the cloud." The picture itself is significant, for it seems to betray a reminiscence, no doubt entirely unconscious on the part of these Priestly writers, of the actual association of the *kebod Yahwe* with the flaming appearance of the dawn when the first rays of the rising sun upon the equinoctial, New Year's Day shine forth from the midst of the cloud upon the eastern horizon. But to accommodate this picture to their doctrine that Yahwe had taken up His permanent abode in the Temple in the form of the *kebod Yahwe*, these Priestly writers had to localize it, to represent their spiritualized conception of the *kebod Yahwe* as confined by the limits of space within the holy of holies of the Temple, as dwelling exactly there, and in no other place, and also as dwelling there permanently and never departing therefrom.[89]

Furthermore, since they now represented the *kebod Yahwe* as dwelling permanently in the holy of holies, and since ancient tradition, based, of course, upon historical fact, told that the " ark of the covenant of Yahwe " likewise stood in the holy of holies, these Priestly writers had no alternative but to associate the ark of tradition with their figure of the *kebod Yahwe*. And since the could not very well represent the latter as contained within the ark, for this would not have comported at all with their conception of the dignity and spirituality of the *kebod Yahwe*, they could depict this association in only one way, viz. that the *kebod Yahwe* was

[88] Num. 9. 15; cf. Ex. 24. 17; 40. 38.
[89] According to Ezekiel 10–11, the departure of the *kebod Yahwe* from the Temple was the sign of the impending destruction of the latter. Similarly the Rabbis of the Tannaitic period and also early Christian writers preserved the tradition that the departure from the second Temple of the Shechinah, likewise through the eastern gate, betokened its impending destruction by the Romans; cf. Jer. Yoma, VI, 43 c; Bab. Yoma, 39 b; also the references cited by Lauterbach, *HUCA*, IV (1927), 184, note 10; Eusebius, *Ecclesiastical History*, III, 8.

enthroned upon the ark. In this, of course, they also had Ezekiel's picture of the enthroned k*e*bod Yahwe as a model. Obviously in this way and by just these processes of reasoning, largely gradual and unconscious though it may all have been, these Priestly writers arrived at the conception of the ark, strange indeed and far removed from its original nature and traditional functions, as a throne of a deity; and, since the k*e*bod Yahwe was purposely and doctrinally regarded as incorporeal and therefore, except upon rare and special occasions, invisible, as an empty throne, or rather, more correctly, as the throne upon which a deity sat, who was invisible to mortals; therefore to mortals it seemed an empty throne.

After all in this process of thus reinterpreting the old ark and representing it as an empty throne these Priestly writers could have experienced no very great difficulty, since this concept was by no means strange to the belief and theology prevalent in their day in the large Semitic world in which Palestine was embedded. For according to Lucian,[90] in the group of eight chief deities whose thrones and images stood in the great Temple at Hierapolis was the sun-god, represented by an empty throne, i. e. one upon which no image of the deity stood; "for," as Lucian says, "the sun and moon are the only divinities that are not sculptured here. On inquiring the reason, I received for answer: Of the other deities it is permitted to make likenesses, because their figures are not known to all men; but the sun and moon are visible to everyone, accordingly there is no reason for delineating them."[91] Unquestionably this reason for not representing the sun by an image, but only by an empty throne, given by Lucian, does not give the real origin and primary cause of this custom, although it may retain some slight reminiscence thereof. But Lucian's statement does seem to imply that this custom was not confined only to the temple at Hierapolis, but was probably observed in most, if not all, Syrian or West-Semitic temples. There is no reason to believe that the Babylonians had this same scruple about depicting the sun-god. In fact the frequent representations in Babylonian pictography

[90] *De Dea Syra*, 34 (ed. Jacobitz, 357).   [91] Tooke's translation, II, 456.

of Shamash seated upon a throne, enveloped in what appears to be a radiant garment and with rays of light streaming forth from behind his shoulders,[92] seem to indicate that the Babylonians regularly depicted both the sun- and the moon-god in this manner. Accordingly it would seem that in their pictures of the k^ebod Yahwe Ezekiel was, more or less consciously, influenced by Babylonian representations of the sun-god, while the Priestly writers were influenced more directly by the West-Semitic practice of representing the sun-god by an empty throne.[93]

But in this enforced association of their picture of the k^ebod Yahwe in the holy of holies with the ark, these Priestly writers were further embarrassed by ancient tradition. On the one hand, they had to accommodate their picture as best they could to the old tradition that the ark was the depository of the two tablets of stone upon which the Ten Commandments were inscribed. It is clear that these two conceptions of the ark have absolutely nothing in common. The ark conceived of as the depository of anything whatsoever was something altogether different than the ark conceived of as a sacred throne. It is self-apparent that it was only that, on the one hand, tradition had inseparably associated the ark with the holy of holies, and that, on the other hand, Priestly tradition or theology now associated the k^ebod Yahwe with the holy of holies in the same way, which brought about this enforced and entirely unnatural and artificial coupling of the ark and the k^ebod Yahwe. Undoubtedly had it not been for this, these Priestly writers would never have represented

[92] Cf. the well-known representation of Shamash upon the Hammurapi-stone, and Jastrow, *Bildermappe zur Religion Babyloniens und Assyriens*, 94.

[93] Whether in thus symbolizing the presence of the k^ebod Yahwe in the holy of holies by an empty throne, these Priestly writers were to any degree conscious of the solar origin of the k^ebod Yahwe, or whether this representation of the k^ebod Yahwe in the manner in which the sun-god was represented at Hierapolis, and apparently also in other West-Semitic temples was purely accidental, or was rather due to the strong Priestly antipathy to the representation of Yahwe by an image of any kind, it is, of course, impossible to determine. Hartmann (*op. cit.* 233), following Reichel and Dibelius, suggests the possibility of Persian influence here also.

Yahwe as enthroned upon the ark, but would instead have represented Him as seated upon an ordinary throne or chair, just as Ezekiel did before them and the author of Dan. 7. 9 after them.

And on the other hand, as we have seen, tradition had likewise associated the k^ebod Yahwe in the Temple on the New Year's Day with a group of heavenly attendants, winged creatures, seraphim or cherubim. Originally, it would seem, they constituted Yahwe's heavenly court, with which He took counsel in fixing the destinies of nations, as well as His attendants and messengers. By the time of Ezekiel they had seemingly, in accordance with developing Jewish theological principles, become conventionalized as the mere, impersonal attendants of Yahwe and bearers of His throne. But apparently they were so integrally associated with the established conception of the k^ebod Yahwe that even the Priestly writers dared not omit them entirely from their picture. However, the extreme and absolute monotheism of these Priestly writers forbade them to conceive of, and much less depict, these cherubim as actual, existent, divine personalities alongside of Yahwe. Accordingly they had but one recourse. Between two to them necessary evils, or rather theological absurdities and impossibilities, they had to choose the less. Accordingly they chose to represent the cherubim, since they could not dispense with them entirely, as conventional figures or images in the holy of holies, either as fixed and inseparable parts of the *kapporet* above the ark,[94] or as in themselves two figures, part of the fixed equipment of the holy of holies in the Temple, standing upon each side of that room, beneath the wings of which the ark was deposited.[95] At least the presence of these images in the holy of holies, contrary though it was to fundamental theological principles of these Priestly writers, was, apparently, not quite so contrary and objectionable as the representation of them as existent, heavenly beings, even though of inferior rank, alongside of,

---

[94] So in Ex. 25. 18 ff. and throughout the Priestly Code.
[95] So in I Ki. 6. 23–28; 8. 6 f.

and thus qualifying the absolute unity of Yahwe, would have been.[96]

It is quite clear from all this that these Priestly writers were probably none too happy in their picture of the k^{e}bod Yahwe in the holy of holies of the Temple at Jerusalem, in its unavoidable and intimate association with the to them basically objectionable, traditional figures of the ark and the cherubim. Unquestionably, had they been able, they would have done away with both ark and cherubim entirely. But tradition, which seemingly strongly colored the popular conception of Yahwe's self-revelation to Israel, and for which too these Priestly writers, with their marked antiquarian instincts, had considerable regard, forbade this. They had to content themselves therefore by reducing the objectionable elements and associations in the picture as much as possible. And this they did by conventionalizing the cherubim and representing them as two images in the holy of holies, in direct association with the ark, and by representing the ark still, though, as we have seen, in unreal and impossible manner, as the depository of the two stone tablets of the Ten Commandments, and likewise, a most unreal and artificial conception, as the base of the empty throne of Yahwe.

But the unreality of this entire procedure and the manifestly basic incompatibility of the ideas involved in this representation of the k^{e}bod Yahwe, with the ark and the cherubim, with fundamental Priestly theological principles, raise the question as to the historic reality of the Priestly account of the ark and its manufacture. Were these Priestly writers actually acquainted with the historic ark? As we have seen, certain internal Biblical evidence, coming from the period shortly after the erection of the second Temple and antedating the composition of the Grundschrift of the Priestly Code and the secondary strata thereof by approximately a century or more, points to the conclusion

---

[96] These Priestly writers felt no doubt that by reducing the four cherubim of Ezekiel, the bearers of the divine throne, to only two, they had lessened somewhat the qualification of Yahwe's absolute unity, implied in this multiplicity of divine figures, even though of inferior rank.

that there was no ark in the second Temple. And, as we have likewise seen, rabbinic tradition is strong that the second Temple contained no ark. In the light of all these facts it is difficult indeed to avoid the conclusion that the picture of the ark which these Priestly writers drew with such elaborate detail, was entirely unhistorical and fanciful, that they had no actual, first-hand knowledge of the historic ark, its appearance, character and functions, and that their picture of it is of little or no value as a source of information as to the original character and purpose of the ark.

C

THE FIRST PERIOD

Accordingly therefore, in our attempts to determine what the ark actually was originally, we are compelled to rely primarily upon the meager evidence furnished by the oldest literary strata of the Bible, supplemented to a certain, slight extent by the information to be gathered from the literature of the second period.

Now the evidence points unmistakably to the conclusion that in the first period of its history the ark was actually looked upon as a deity. Not only by the Philistines was the ark so regarded,[97] but by Israel also, for it was taken into battle against the Philistines for the express purpose, "that it may come among us and deliver us from the hand of our enemies."[98] In this function of the ark significant parallels from the practice of other Semitic peoples are not lacking. Ġadîmah, the Laḫmite king at Ḥîrah, used to carry two idols, aḍ-Ḍâribân, (literally, "the two smiters," or, perhaps more exactly and significantly, "the two givers of victory") into battle with him.[99] Even the Philistines themselves carried the images of their gods with them into battle, and in his great victory over them these images were captured by David.[100]

[97] Cf. I Sam. 4. 6–8 (especially in the LXX version).
[98] I Sam. 4. 3.
[99] Osiander, "Studien über die vorislâmische Religion der Araber," *ZDMG*, VII (1853), 501.
[100] II Sam. 5. 21. For additional instances of this practice among the Semites, cf. Gressmann, *Mose und seine Zeit*, 233.

Likewise in its experience of capture by the Philistines and sojourn as a trophy of victory in their land, the ark has significant Semitic parallels. Among the Babylonians and Assyrians and the various peoples with whom they contended, the carrying off of the images of the gods of the vanquished by the victors, was a common occurrence. The classic instance is, of course, the capture of the statue of the Babylonian goddess Nanâ by the Elamites and its recovery by Ašurbanapal sixteen hundred and thirty-five years later and restoration to its old temple at Erech.[101] The explanatory statement given by the Assyrian king is significant. It was not that the Elamites had been more powerful than the Babylonians, or that the goddess herself had been weak and unable to protect herself or her people against their enemy, but that she had been enraged against her own people and so had permitted herself to be carried away to a strange land. Even among her enemies, impliedly, just like the ark of Israel, she was still a powerful deity; only, presumably, her blessings were now bestowed upon the people among whom she was dwelling, her former enemies, while her old worshipers, deprived of her presence, and therefore without divine protection and rendered correspondingly weak and helpless, became the ready prey of their foes. Manifestly the capture of the image or cult object of the deity of an enemy, served a double purpose. Not only was it a trophy of victory, but even more, its possession rendered the enemy correspondingly stronger and its old worshipers correspondingly weaker. That similar ideas obtained among the pre-Islamic Arabs may be inferred from a statement of Nuwairî that four Himyarite princes, the sons of As'ad b. 'Amr, undertook an expedition to carry off the sacred black stone, the Ka'aba, in order to set it up in a sanctuary which they contemplated erecting in Ṣan'â; but they were defeated by the Banu Kinânah.[102] Not improbably the Philistines expected the ark to function in their midst in some such favorable manner, and were therefore doubly distressed when they

---

[101] Rawlinson, *The Cuneiform Inscriptions of Western Asia*, V, 6, col. VI, 107–128.
[102] Osiander, *op. cit.*, 478.

discovered that its presence among them was inimical to them to an extreme degree. And apparently the presence of the ark in their midst brought blessing to the household of Abinadab and all the inhabitants of Kiryat Yearim,[103] just as, so we are told explicitly, it brought blessing to the inmates of the house of Obed-Edom, in which it stood likewise.[104]

The character of the ark as a divine object is likewise attested significantly by the taboo inherent in it. Even to touch it without warrant, although for the most worthy and devout purpose, entailed death. Uzza died because he had ventured to lay his hand upon it in order to steady it, when it seemed that it might slip from the wagon.[105] And the clan of Yechoniah, of the inhabitants of Beth-Shemesh, suffered the loss of seventy members because they had dared to examine the ark too closely, and perhaps even to look into it, and had thereby violated the taboo associated with it.[106]

---

[103] I Sam. 7. 1; II Sam. 6. 3.
[104] II Sam. 6. 12.
[105] II Sam. 6. 6f.
[106] I Sam. 6. 19, emended in accordance with the more correct LXX text. This passage has never, so far as I can see, been interpreted quite correctly. H. P. Smith (*Samuel; International Critical Commentary* series, 48 f.), followed by Budde (*Samuel;* in Marti's *Hand-Commentar* series, 46) and Gressmann (*Die Lade Jahves*, 19), explains the misfortune of the Bne Yechoniah as brought upon them by Yahwe because they did not rejoice with the rest of the inhabitants of Beth Shemesh when they beheld the ark. But why should they not have rejoiced equally with their fellow-townsmen upon this occasion, unless there was some specific reason for their not doing so? And since the approach of the ark to Beth Shemesh was undoubtedly the first contact of the Bne Yechoniah with it, whatever reason they may have had for not joining in the celebration of their fellow-townsmen could not have arisen before, but must have arisen after this event. Plain common sense therefore indicates that the misfortune which befell them in the loss of seventy of the members of their clan could not have been because they did not rejoice when they beheld the ark, but, just the reverse, this misfortune was itself the cause of their not being able to rejoice along with the other inhabitants of their village.

Now it should be noticed that in v. 13 ויראו is followed by the direct object, את הארון, while in v. 19 ראו is followed by the preposition ב, ראו בארון. ראה ב״ means " to look at a thing fixedly, to examine it closely " (Gen. 21. 16; 34. 1; Is. 66. 24; Cant. 6. 11; Eccl. 2. 1; 11. 4), then " to take due notice of, to have regard for " (Gen. 29. 32; Num. 11. 15; I Sam. 1. 11; II Sam. 16. 12; Ps. 37. 4; 128. 5). Here it must mean, " they examined it closely," i.e. they handled

Manifestly it was just because it was a deity that the ark could bring blessing to the household, town or nation in which it was dwelling, whether temporarily or permanently, and where it was treated with due regard and proper ceremonial, as well as inflict punishment whenever the proper limits of its taboo were violated. The anticipation of blessing from having the ark with him, based no doubt upon reports which had come to him of the prosperity of the people of Kiryat Yearim, and later of that of Obed-Edom, must have been one of the primary motives actuating David in his purpose to bring the ark up to Jerusalem, just as the fear of the ark, based upon the unhappy fate of Uzza, deterred him for a time from carrying out his plan. It was likewise because the ark was regarded as a deity that it was thought able to give its people victory in battle, to select the way it wished to go and to lead its people along the otherwise unknown way which they had to travel, and bring them in safety to their ultimate goal, which it, or rather the deity associated with it, had promised to them. Presumably, too, the ark could discharge many other functions, of which we have no record, but which were the functions thought to be usually discharged by a deity and to redound to the blessing of its people.

it, for it was no doubt an object of which they had heard frequently in the past, and perhaps had even heard of its marvellous exploits in the land of the Philistines; and now that it had come among them, naturally they sought to satisfy their curiosity and see for themselves just what this ark was. Unaware of the taboo qualities of the ark, they did not hesitate to treat it too familiarly, to handle it unceremoniously, and not at all improbably, they even ventured to look inside it to see what might be there. Consequently they suffered the same fate as did Uzza, for venturing to touch the ark. Those who dared to examine the ark too closely, and especially to touch it, died automatically. It was no violation of the taboo of the ark, to look at it, as v. 13 indicates; but it was a violation of the taboo to examine the ark too closely, with all the treatment that this implies. We can well understand therefore, why, as v. 20 states, the people of Beth Shemesh feared to keep the ark in their town, for there could be no telling who would be the next, even though innocent, victim of the violation of the taboo associated with it. We must accordingly translate v. 19, not as do Smith, Budde and Gressmann, " The Bne Yechoniah did not rejoice with the men of Beth Shemesh *when they beheld* the ark," but " *because they examined* the ark."

THE BOOK OF THE COVENANT

Moreover, all the evidence indicates that the ark, or the deity of the ark, was identified with Yahwe. The sanctuary at Shiloh, ministered to by a Levitical family, was a Yahwe shrine. The ark was there known apparently as the ארון יהוה, "the ark of Yahwe." And the Philistines themselves, according to tradition, identified the deity of the ark with the god who had brought Israel up from Egypt.[107] The implication too of the tradition recorded in I Sam. 5. 1–5, of the prostration of the image of Dagon before the ark, is likewise that the ark is a divine object or deity of character similar to that of the image of the Philistine deity, but of course of superior power and authority.

Most significant of all perhaps is the legend recorded in I Sam. 3. As is recognized by practically all scholars, this chapter belongs to a literary stratum somewhat later than I Sam. 4–6, and therefore quite naturally it seems to show some evidence of a slightly more advanced theology. None the less Yahwe is here associated with the ark in the most intimate and significant manner. The legend tells that while lying at night in the place in the sanctuary where the ark stood, Samuel hears Yahwe calling to him. Presumably it was in anticipation of some such occurrence that Samuel slept in this spot, no doubt having been assigned to this task by Eli. For the same reason, as we have seen,[108] Ex. 33. 11 tells that while Moses would return to the camp from the "tent of meeting," the youthful Joshua, Moses' apprentice, according to the J tradition, remained always within the tent and never went forth from it. The purpose here, too, was manifestly to receive the oracle. For this could never be anticipated; and whenever Yahwe would choose to speak, some one qualified by technical training must be present to receive the message. So here, the youthful Samuel, likewise the apprentice of Eli, sleeps in the room where the ark is, while Eli, the old priest, sleeps in his

---

[107] I Sam. 4. 8b. This passage is undoubtedly not original. All the more therefore it indicates that until a time later than the actual composition of the earliest stratum of I Sam. 4–6 the ark itself as a deity was identified with Yahwe.

[108] "The Oldest Document, &c.," *HUCA*, IV (1927), 119 ff.

accustomed bed, in order that he too might receive the oracle whenever Yahwe should choose to speak.

The presumption is strong, therefore, that the oracle of Yahwe here was associated with the ark, that, in other words, the narrative in its original form implied that Yahwe spoke from out the ark. It is true that v. 10 says explicitly that Yahwe came and took His place and then called the third time to Samuel, implying thereby that Yahwe was not present regularly in this room or portion of the sanctuary, but came thither only for the explicit purpose of calling to Samuel, and furthermore came and went away and then came again, each time that He called to Samuel. This procedure seems hardly natural or plausible. On the basis of v. 10 Smith [109] and Budde [110] would emend v. 4 to read, ויתיצב יהוה ויקרא, But it would be more plausible and much simpler to regard ויבא יהוה ויתיצב in v. 10 as a late, theological insertion, and the original reading, just as in v. 4 and again in v. 6, the simple ויקרא יהוה. In fact v. 6 seems to imply that just this was the original reading, rather than that proposed by Smith and Budde. But if this was indeed the original reading,

[109] *Op. cit.*, 25 ff.
[110] *Op. cit.*, 28. It is likewise easier to account for the insertion of ויבא יהוה ויתיצב in v. 10, on the basis of theological motivation, than it would be to account for the reverse procedure of a suppression, whether purposed or not, of an original ויבא יהוה ויתיצב in vv. 4 and 6. For we can readily understand that a later age, during the second period of the history of the ark, would take exception to the idea of Yahwe dwelling within the ark and speaking from out it. This was too crass and primitive, and smacked too much of the representation of Yahwe or the symbolization of His presence by a concrete, image-like object, to be acceptable to the prophetic theology which dominated this second period. As we have intimated, it must have been just because of the development of this prophetic conception of Yahwe, that the conception of the ark as the receptacle of the two tablets of stone developed. By the insertion of ויבא יהוה ויתיצב in v. 10, late glossators imagined that they had corrected the impression originally conveyed by this and vv. 4 and 6, that Yahwe spoke from out the ark. The insertion of these words, they believed, no doubt, implied that Yahwe came from afar, wherever that might be, presumably in heaven, to speak with Samuel. In quite the same way and from the same standpoint the J Code occasionally represents Yahwe as descending from somewhere on high, presumably from heaven (וירד יהוה, Gen. 11. 5; Ex. 19. 20; Num. 11. 25; וירד יהוה ויעמד, Num. 12. 5; and especially, וירד יהוה ויתיצב, Ex. 34. 5).

then it and the entire narrative imply beyond all possibility of doubt that Yahwe was actually present all the time in the room in which Samuel was sleeping, and that, just as we have suggested, Samuel was appointed by Eli to sleep in this room regularly, since Eli himself was apparently too old and feeble for this constant and exacting service, to receive the oracle whenever Yahwe would choose to speak. And of course Yahwe could be present in only one particular place or object in this room, viz. the ark, precisely as the explicit mention of the presence of the ark in this room in v. 3 implies. This chapter accordingly furnishes very strong and illuminating proof, not only of the direct association of Yahwe with the ark, but that actually in this first period of its history Yahwe was thought to actually reside within the ark.

Furthermore, the very name ארון, "box, casket" implies as various scholars have remarked, that the ark must have been primarily a container; i. e. in itself it could hardly have been regarded as the deity, as Yahwe, but must rather have contained, or at least have been thought to contain something, which was either regarded as Yahwe Himself, or else, what practically amounts to the same thing, as being the object in which Yahwe was thought to reside. This is confirmed by the established tradition of the second period of the history of the ark, that in it the two stone tablets of the Decalogue were deposited. It is confirmed still further by the interpretation of I Sam. 6. 19 which we have proposed, viz. that the clan of Yechoniah of Beth Shemesh examined the ark closely, and perhaps even looked into it, of course to see what was inside, and therefore were so sorely smitten by Yahwe. Our task therefore is now to determine, if possible, what the actual contents of the ark, so intimately associated with Yahwe, may have been.

In this phase of the question as to the form and nature of the ark, Semitic religious belief and practice offer striking and significant parallels. Sanchuniathon records that Agroueros or Agrotes, apparently, to judge from the names, an agricultural deity, had a wooden statue which was much venerated, and a shrine (or portable temple), drawn about in Phoenicia by yokes of oxen.[111] Presumably this last was an object somewhat similar to the ark.

Far more striking in its parallelism with the ark is a peculiar structure which seems to play more or less of the rôle of a cult object among the Ruwala, an important and powerful tribe of the present-day Anazeh group of Bedouin tribes. The description of it, given by Musil,[112] is as follows; "The Ruwala have a structure made out of thin wooden boards, decorated with ostrich feathers, which is fastened upon the baggage-saddle of a camel. It is called *abu ẓhûr al-markab*. Only the Ruwala possess this. No other tribe has anything like it. As they believe, the *abu ẓhûr* comes from Ruweil (the eponymous ancestor of the Ruwala) and is called *abuẓ hûr* (*pater aeterni saeculi*) because it is passed on from generation to generation through the ages. *Abu ẓhûr* is the visible focus ... of all the tribes of the *zana*-Moslems. Whoever has it in his possession is prince of all these tribes, and they are obligated to follow him in battle. Every year a white camel is sacrificed before it, with the words, 'This is thy sacrifice, O Abu Ẓhûr!,' and its blood is sprinkled upon the corner posts of the structure. In this *abu ẓhûr* Allah takes pleasure in abiding and imparts directions to the tribe through external signs. Ofttimes the ostrich-feathers are supposed to tremble, although there may be no wind. Ofttimes the structure is believed to bow itself unceasingly to the right. This signifies *ḳudrat min allâh*, 'the power of God.' ... If the camel bearing the *abu ẓhûr* begins to move, the entire tribe follows it; where the *abu ẓhûr* lets itself down, there the camp is set up. Whenever the Ruwala are threatened by a powerful enemy and fear defeat (but only then) they bring the *abu ẓhûr*, and with it at their head they attack the enemy."

The points of similarity and manifest relationship between this strange object and the various Biblical traditions about the ark are almost startling. It too has the power of selecting the road it wishes to take, by driving the camel

---

[111] Cf. Cory, *Ancient Fragments*, 9.
[112] *Die Kultur*, XI (1910), 8 f., quoted from Hartmann, "Zelt und Lade," *ZAW*, 37 (1917–1918), 220f.

which bears it irresistibly onwards. It too leads its people through the desert and determines their nightly campingplaces by causing the camel bearing it to kneel, implying thereby that there it desires to stop and remain for the night. It too imparts oracles and, in the interest of its tribe, declares future events. It too goes into battle with its people and gives them victory over its and their enemies. And not this alone, for it does not go into every battle, but only into those battles where the danger is urgent and the security of the tribe is greatly imperilled. Just this was the procedure with the ark; for it was not taken into the first battle with the Philistines, where, seemingly, the tribes of Israel felt quite confident of victory. Only after this first defeat, and when the danger impending had become fully apparent, did they fall back upon their last resort, in which, clearly, they had implicit confidence, and bring the ark with them into battle. And, most significant of all these points of contact with the ark, Allah is thought to reside in the *abu ẓhûr*, if not permanently, then upon occasions when the tribe has need of him and his presence with them, just as, as we have seen, Yahwe too was at first thought to reside in the ark; and every year a sacrifice, and a major sacrifice at that, since it consists of a white camel, is offered to the *abu ẓhûr*, or to the deity associated with it, and the blood thereof is sprinkled upon the cornerposts of the peculiar object, with the significant words, "This is thy sacrifice, O Abu Ẓhûr."

And this parallelism becomes still more significant when we realize that Musil failed to grasp the full significance of this peculiar object and the rôle which it played in the life of the tribe, and particularly in its warfare, having been misled somewhat by the popular but incorrect interpretation of the name *abu ẓhûr*. This was more clearly recognized by Hartmann and Torczyner.[113] The latter scholar quotes a verse,

[113] "Die Bundeslade und die Anfänge der Religion Israels," *Festschrift zum 50 jährigen Bestehen der Hochschule für die Wissenschaft des Judentums*, 265.

recorded by Curtiss,[114] as having been communicated to him by a Ruwala-tribesman,

> Abu ed-Duhûr will come unfailingly
> To help those who put on their equipment for war;
> And through him their horses become fear-inspiring.

As Curtiss has pointed out, *abu ẓhûr*, according to these verses, plays exactly the rôle of a tribal deity, and particularly a deity who gives his tribesmen victory in war. In all likelihood *abu ẓhûr* was originally the actual name of the tribal deity of the Ruwala, which has, however, under the influence of official Islam, superficial though it be with the Bedouin tribesmen, been half forgotten with the passage of time, and lingers on chiefly, if not entirely, in its association with this peculiar tribal cult- or war-object.

In one other respect Musil's description of this object, based upon the information given to him, was somewhat inexact, in that it was claimed that this was the only object of its kind, and that no other people possessed anything like it. The full name of this object was communicated to Musil as *abu ẓhûr al-markab*. The consideration given to the very important first half of the name has tended to detract somewhat from the consideration which the second half likewise merits.

Markab connotes in Arabic a vehicle of any kind used for transportation, whether wagon, boat or beast of burden. Burckhardt[115] is our authority for the fact that the Bedouin

---

[114] *Ursemitische Religion im Volksleben des heutigen Orients*, XV. Moreover, according to Canaan ("Mohammedan Saints and Sanctuaries in Palestine," *JPOS*, IV [1924], 83), Abu ed-Dhûr is the name of "a rock, situated on the left side of the carriage road from Jerusalem to Jericho, after passing 'ên el-Ḥôḍ. This rock has a widespread reputation for the cure of backache. After a patient has rubbed his back against the rock, he places a stone on it. When last I saw this 'father of rocks,' he was loaded with a large heap of stones. He is not assigned at present to any *welî*, and I can not explain its widespread therapeutic use, except by assuming that it may have been once connected in some way with a holy man or object of worship." Doubtless had Canaan been familiar with the *abu ẓhûr* of the Ruwala, and the evidence pointing to a former tribal deity Abu ed-Duhûr, he would have associated this rock with him.

[115] *Notes on the Bedouins and Wahábys*, 82 f.

tribes of the North Arabian desert actually possess several such objects, or at least did so a century ago. He says, " Some of the Aeneze chiefs use, in time of war, what may perhaps be styled the 'battle banner'; for it is never displayed but in decisive and important actions, where the fall or the loss of it is regarded as a signal of defeat. This standard is of two sorts, one called *merkeb* (مركب, or the 'ship'), consisting in two stands of wood, about six or seven feet high;... These are placed one opposite to the other on a camel's back, so that above there is not more than a span's distance between them; but below they are sufficiently separated for a person to sit in the midst on a saddle, and guide the camel: the upper part of this standard is covered with black ostrich feathers.

"The other sort of banner is called *'otfe* (عطفة); this consists of two side pieces of board, of an oblong square form, about five feet high, ornamented like the other with ostrich feathers. Such is now used by the *Teyar*, the chief of *Would Aly*... *En Ibsmeyr* and *Ibn Fadhel* have each a *merkeb*. The guide of the camel, that carries either a *merkeb* or an *'otfe*, is never an adult free-born Arab, but a boy, an old woman, or a slave; for it is thought beneath the dignity of a man to sing or howl the cry called زغاريت, with which the guide animates those who accompany the standard to battle. All the horsemen assemble around it; and the principal efforts of both parties are directed against the respective *merkeb* or *'otfe* of the enemy. A captured banner is borne in triumph to the tent of the victorious sheikh."

According to this description of Burckhardt there are two varieties of this peculiar object, one called *merkeb* and the other *'otfe*. Seemingly they differ only in form and outward appearance, but serve exactly the same function. Burckhardt apparently heard nothing from his informers about Allah or any tribal deity residing in this object, nor of its being used for purposes of divination. He heard of only one function which it discharged, viz. that of the tribal banner or palladium in battle, however not used indiscriminately for this purpose, but carried by the tribe only into the most important and decisive engagements. Its presence there was obviously assumed to ensure victory to its tribe. On the other hand Burckhardt's description adds one significant element, totally lacking in that of Musil, and apparently not heard of by him in connection with the *abu zhûr al-markab* of the Ruwala, viz. that of the rider, whether boy, old woman or slave, in the *merkeb*, whose task was by his cries to spur on the warriors to extreme efforts. Finally, Burckhardt's description establishes with certainty that the *abu zhûr al-markab* of the Ruwala is not, as they claimed, the only object of its kind, but that similar objects are, or at least were quite recently, possessed by other tribes or tribal chieftains.

Still further light is shed upon this strange object, and particularly upon that of the Ruwala, by Wetzstein.[116] "Should it develop that they become convinced that victory can not be won except by extreme measures, they have still in the 'Otfa a final and in fact a very drastic means of inflaming the battle-spirit. The 'Otfa is a lattice-work object, made of strong wood, four-cornered, of greater length than width, and almost oval in shape, which is fastened upon the back of a strong, decorated camel. The older the 'Otfa is, the more it possesses the qualifications for serving as the palladium of its people; that of the Ruwala, one of the large 'Anesa-tribes of the Syrian desert, of which I made a drawing in 1860 in the tent of the tribal battle-leader, is said to be hundreds of years old. Before the beginning of the battle an especially handsome and reputable woman or maiden, if possible the one of highest rank within the tribe, adorned as a bride, unveiled, and, what has a peculiarly disturbing effect upon the Arabs, with hair flying loose and neck laid bare, mounts the 'Otfa, rides in front of the first battle-line and halts before the elite of the army, the youth of the tribe, in order to direct toward them the Intichâ, i. e. the solemn charge either to win the victory or to die. This consists of the little word liainêki, 'for thy two eyes!' Thereupon the 'Otfa advances upon the enemy and the battle begins. The greatest slaughter naturally takes place in the neighborhood of the

---

[116] *Verhandlungen der Berliner Gesellschaft für Anthropologie*, X (1878), 389; quoted from Hartmann, " Zelt und Lade," *ZAW*, 37 (1917–1918), 219f.

'Oṭfa, towards the capture and defence of which the main efforts of both sides are directed. During the combat the occupant of the 'Oṭfa, standing erect and turning now here, now there, spurs her fellow-tribesmen on with glance and gesture, with loud challenge and calling individual warriors by name, with praise and blame and the trilling sounds of the Zaġrûta (the customary cries of joy of the attendants of the bride at weddings). Not infrequently the entire body of male youth has fallen beside the ‚Oṭfa. Likewise it is often captured, a fact which is remembered as a lasting humiliation for many generations. However, the beautiful woman, captured with the 'Otfa, is always treated honorably, and is released for a ransom, but one of very great amount. The ‚Oṭfa remains as the trophy of the victor, if it is not recaptured by an attack upon the enemy's camp."

This description of Wetzstein adds some significant information to our knowledge of these peculiar objects. In the first place it confirms the fact that the *abu ẓhûr al-markab* of the Ruwala is not unique, but that there are, or at least were, among the Bedouin tribes of the Syrian desert other like objects. In the second place it gives further information about the particular object of the Ruwala. Significantly this object, which Musil heard designated by the descriptive title *al-markab*, Wetzstein must have heard called 'otfe. This indicates that the two names are apparently used interchangeably, without the distinction between them which Burckhardt recorded. Furthermore, the older an 'otfe is, the more respect it enjoys, presumably because it is thought to be therefore more powerful and effective. That of the Ruwala seems to have been regarded as unusually old and therefore to have enjoyed a particular reputation and veneration. According to Wetzstein only a beautiful and highly respected woman occupies the 'otfe, whereas according to Burckhardt, this is instead a boy, an old woman or a slave. There is no reason to question the reliability of both accounts. The facts in the case seem to be that the customary occupant of the 'otfe is a young woman, who plays the rôle of a battle-maiden, spurring on fellow-tribesmen by her cries, her gestures and glances, and even not infrequently by shouts of praise or rebuke for this or that individual warrior. Not infrequently, however, this rôle may be filled by an old woman, a boy or a slave; only never an actual warrior. An ʿoṭfe captured in battle, is retained by the captors, so long as possible, as a trophy of victory. But, as is but natural, the conquered tribe makes every possible effort to regain its palladium, and until it succeeds in doing this, it feels itself humiliated and dishonored.

Further information of some significance about the ʿoṭfe of the Ruwala is given by Blunt.[117] "The last thing loaded by Ibn Shaalán's people was the *uttfa*, a gigantic camel-hówdah used by the Roála whenever they expect a pitched battle, and then only. It is a huge cage of bamboo covered with ostrich feathers, and probably as old as the date of their first coming from Nejd, for ostriches are not found, I believe, north of Jebel Shammar. A delúl carries the *uttfa*, in which a girl is placed, whose business it is to sing during the fight, and encourage the combatants by her words. She needs to be stout-hearted as well as stout-lunged, for the battle generally groups itself round her, in attack and defence. The Roála have a superstitious feeling about her defence, and the enemy a corresponding desire to capture her, for it is a belief that with the loss of the *uttfa* the Roála tribe would perish. Formerly, each large Bedouin tribe had one of these; but now, perhaps from a scarcity of ostrich feathers and the difficulty of renewing them, the *uttfa* and the custom attached to it have disappeared, except among the Roála and, I believe, the Ibn Haddal.[118] To-day it was carried empty on the back of a fine she-camel."

This description of the ʿoṭfe of the Ruwala confirms that of Wetzstein, and likewise much of the general description of the ʿoṭfe and *merkab* given by Burckhardt. It also confirms the statement of Wetzstein that the regular occupant of the ʿoṭfe is a maiden of the tribe. Perhaps this was the regular

[117] *The Bedouins of the Euphrates*, 351.
[118] Lady Blunt adds the note that Palgrave mentions its existence among the Ajman, a tribe east of Jebel Shammar. However, she fails to give the reference for this, and I have not succeeded in locating it in Palgrave, *Central and Eastern Arabia*.

practice among the Ruwala, while among other tribes her place might be taken, at least occasionally, by an old woman, a boy or a slave, as Burckhardt records. The extreme regard and veneration with which the 'oṭfe is treated is evidenced by the character of the camel which bears it, and also by the fact that when the tribe is about to set out on a journey the 'oṭfe is the last object packed up. Apparently the loading of the 'oṭfe upon the back of the particular camel designated to carry it might well serve as the signal for the tribe to set out.

Lady Blunt's description also confirms Wetzstein's statement with regard to the high age of the particular 'oṭfe of the Ruwala. Apparently Lady Blunt regarded the decoration of ostrich feathers as essential to the 'oṭfe, for she accounts for the gradual disappearance of this institution from among the various tribes by the assumption that this is because of the difficulty of securing sufficient ostrich feathers to keep the old 'oṭfes in proper repair and to make new ones. This would accord somewhat with Musil's statement that it was through the waving of these ostrich feathers, particularly when there was no wind, that the deity associated with this particular 'oṭfe was thought to impart oracular information. But this assumption of Lady Blunt is groundless; for, on the one hand, were it correct, we would expect to find the institution of the 'oṭfe, with all the peculiar beliefs associated with it, far more general among the Bedouin tribes living to the south of the Syrian desert, where the ostrich is more common;[118a] and, quite significantly, the 'oṭfe seems to be almost, if not entirely, unknown in that region. And, on the other hand, we shall have ample evidence that ostrich feathers are not at all essential to certain objects closely related to the 'oṭfe. The gradual disappearance of the 'oṭfe from among the Bedouin tribes, has, as we shall see shortly, a simpler, more natural and probable, and also for this study more significant reason.

Additional light is shed upon the nature and function of the 'oṭfe by Rogers.[119] " The sheikhs of the 'Anazy tribes

[118a] According to Lawrence (*Revolt in the Desert*, 59) the ostrich is plentiful still today in the territory of the Sherarat, in the desert east of Tebuk. (Tebuk is on the railway almost due east of the southernmost point of the Sinaitic Peninsula).
[119] In *The Academy* of Mar. 31, 1883, 221 f., writing from Cairo.

say that in ancient times every tribe had its 'Atfah, which was regarded as the repository of its valour and honour, and was only made use of on occasions of unusually serious importance. When a tribe went to war with a powerful opponent, the 'Atfah was placed on a strong and handsome camel, and was gaily and gorgeously decorated with ostrich-feathers, carpets, and embroidery work, and was surrounded by a band of warriors selected from among the bravest men of the tribe. In some tribes it was customary for a virgin, the daughter of one of the sheikhs, to take her seat under the canopy, and, by her singing, to incite the men to acts of bravery. Every effort was made and every precaution taken to prevent its falling into the hands of the enemy; and, if the men engaged in fighting in another part of the field, or told off for the protection of the flocks or of the tents, perceived that the 'Atfah was in danger, they would leave their occupation, abandoning everything to rally round the mysterious emblem for its protection; for, if lost, the tribe was disgraced, and a new 'Atfah could not be made until after a victory over the enemy who had possessed himself of the original and the recovery of a remnant—be it ever so small a portion—of the old wooden framework. The captured 'Atfah could not be used by the victorious tribe, and it was therefore generally destroyed after capture. This custom accounts for the fact that of all the numerous tribes in the Syrian deserts only two now possess an 'Atfah."

This account is of extreme importance. In the first place it gives further confirmation to the conclusion that the customary, though by no means invariable, occupant of the 'otfe was a maiden. And in the second place it too records that at one time the institution of the 'otfe was quite common among Bedouin tribes, and accounts for its gradual disappearance, not by supposition, as did Lady Blunt, but by a fact of much significance. A new 'otfe could not be made indiscriminately to replace an old one which had been captured or destroyed in battle. The capture of an 'otfe was regarded as such a supreme calamity that the tribe did not hesitate at the most extreme efforts and sacrifices to protect it. The tribe whose 'oṭfe had been captured in battle was regarded as, and felt itself disgraced and humiliated. Not until it had regained its old 'oṭfe through victory in battle, could it hold its head high once more. A new 'oṭfe could be made only with at least a remnant of the old 'oṭfe as its nucleus. A captured 'oṭfe could not be used by its captors. Therefore, in order to forestall all possibility of its former tribe regaining it, or at least a portion of it, from which a new 'oṭfe might be made, symbolic of the restored power of the now conquered tribe, a captured 'oṭfe was usually destroyed. The inevitable result of such a practice must have been the gradual disappearance of the 'oṭfe from among the Bedouin tribes. We can easily understand therefore why during the second half of the 19th century but one or two 'oṭfes should still be in existence.

But the question arises here, Why, if the old 'oṭfe were captured, could not a new one be made to replace it, unless at least a fragment of the old 'oṭfe was used as the nucleus for it? An answer, altogether natural and of deep significance suggests itself. We have seen that, according to Musil's direct account, Allah was believed to reside in the 'oṭfe, if not permanently, at least occasionally. Moreover, other important evidence links this particular 'oṭfe of the Ruwala with Abu ed-Duhûr, apparently the old, half-forgotten, eponymous deity of this tribe. It is altogether probable that every ancient 'oṭfe had similar associations, that it was regarded, in earlier and more primitive stages of its development, as the symbol, or even as the actual container of the tribal deity. In such case, its capture in battle would mean nothing other than this deity's capture by his enemies. It would imply, on the one hand, his own weakness and impotence in comparison with the enemy tribe and its deity; and on the other hand, it would imply that his old tribe was now without divine protection, was therefore in truth weak and humiliated. We can well understand, on the basis of this hypothesis, why a tribe would spare no effort and sacrifice to prevent the capture of its 'oṭfe, and would even leave its cattle and its tents, of course with the women and children in them, unprotected and at the mercy of the enemy, in order to protect its ʿoṭfe against capture.

Above all, on the basis of this assumption of an original association of ʿoṭfe and tribal deity, we can understand why a new ʿoṭfe could be made only with a portion, no matter how small, of the old one serving as a nucleus. For the old ʿoṭfe must have been charged in its every part with the spirit or indwelling of a deity. And this could be communicated to the new ʿoṭfe only by contact with the old one, and particularly if a portion of the old ʿoṭfe, charged with this divine essence, were built into the new one.[120] From this nucleus this divine essence spread until it completely permeated the new ʿoṭfe, and endowed it with a divinity and power equal to, and in fact identical with that of the old ʿoṭfe. Accordingly the complete destruction of an ʿoṭfe by its captors, made it absolutely impossible for its old owners to replace it. It must have meant to them and to their neighbors that they were a tribe entirely without divine protection, that they were therefore weak and impotent, held in light esteem by the surrounding tribes, and themselves disspirited and humiliated. It goes without saying too, just as Rogers states, that a captured ʿoṭfe could not be used by its captors. For, on the one hand, it had been the tribal deity of their enemies, and therefore could not be expected to bestow its divine help and blessing upon its former foes; and on the other hand, of what value would its help and blessing be to its captors, since in comparison with their own tribal deity it had proved of inferior strength and powerless to protect even itself from capture? To its captors it was of no avail whatever, but it might, despite its unquestionable divine nature, be destroyed by them with impunity. From such an impotent deity they had naught to fear.[121]

[120] Cf. Robertson Smith, *The Religion of the Semites*,² index under *holiness* and *taboo*.

[121] Some such condition as this may account for the otherwise almost inexplicable fact that the tribes which came forth from Egypt adopted the worship of the Yahwe of the mountain in the desert, a deity up to that time apparently worshiped only by the Kenites, and certainly unknown to and not worshiped by them, as all the Biblical traditions, with the single exception of that of J,

The most recent account of the ʻoṭfe [122] adds nothing to what has already been learned with regard to it; but inasmuch as it confirms a number of important facts, already elucidated, as well as for the sake of completeness, it may be cited here. It deals only with the oft-mentioned ʻoṭfe of the

agree. Not impossibly the conditions which caused these tribes to settle in Egypt, or the misfortunes attendant upon them during their sojourn there, had made them lose faith in the strength and protective power of their former tribal deities. Not improbably they had even lost their old, tribal cult-objects or deity-symbols, comparable in every way, as we shall see shortly, to the present-day ʻoṭfe, and so felt themselves entirely without a god of their own. Moses enheartened them with the message of a new god, who would adopt them as his people and take them under his protection. And when the power of this deity and his good-will towards them were manifested by the discomfiture and humiliation of the Egyptians and their gods, they were convinced of the truth of Moses' message and were ready to enter into covenant relations with this new and unquestionably powerful deity.

Similarly too the tribe of Dan must have been convinced by repeated defeat and the gradual decimation of their once powerful tribe at the hands of their Emorite or Philistine enemies, that their former tribal deity was unable to protect and prosper them. Quite probably too their old tribal cult-object, whatever it may have been, had been captured and destroyed, so that they now felt themselves entirely without a god of their own. At any rate their situation was so precarious that they had to resort to the desperate expedient of forsaking their old, tribal territory and migrating to a new home far to the north. On their way they stole the household idol of Micah, the Ephraimite, and adopted it as their new deity and tribal cult-object (Jud. 17–18). They could have been prompted to this last and altogether unusual and desperate act only if at the moment they actually had no tribal god and cult-object of their own. This extraordinary condition can be explained most satisfactorily by the above assumption of the capture and destruction of their former tribal cult-object, whatever it may have been.

This evidence suffices to prove that Jeremiah was wrong, even as far as Israel was concerned, in the implication of his rhetorical question, " Can a nation change its gods? " (2. 11). For his own day, with its large and powerful nations, each with its own elaborate pantheon, his question may have applied. But for ancient Israel, with its simple, primitive, tribal society, and for other Semitic peoples, dwelling upon the same tribal plane of social organization, the loss of old gods with the capture and destruction of old tribal cult-objects or god-symbols, and the consequent, eventual adoption by them of the worship of new and presumably more powerful deities, was by no means an impossible and unheard of, nor even uncommon procedure.

[122] Leachman, "A Journey in North-Eastern Arabia," *Geographical Journal*, 37 (1911), 267.

Ruwala. "As a rule the mounted men marched in front, behind them coming the thelul riders, while in the middle of them, on a picked 'thelul' (dromedary) was the 'Mirkab' of the Roalla. This consists of a frame covered with black ostrich feathers, in which a maiden from the sheikh's family rides in battle, exhorting the combatants to deeds of valour. In former times the 'Mirkab' was a familiar sight in Beduin warfare, but

> In a very recent work (Seabrook, *Adventures in Arabia*, 85 ff.), published in 1927, after this article was written, the following description of the '*otfe* occurs (although the name '*otfe* is not used). "Pitched battles still occur occasionally among the prouder Bedouin tribes ...... The time and place are appointed. The opposing forces arrive panoplied, with all their tents and women, and set up their camps in full view of each other. Personal tournaments ...... often precede the battle.
>
> "Instead of a flag or banner, each tribe has for its standard a sort of human oriflamme—an enormous throne fitted to a camel's back, a big, square litter with a canopy, completely covered with ostrich plumes dyed in brilliant colors. On the day of battle this throne is placed on a giant camel, with three or four of the most beautiful marriageable virgins of the tribe, dressed in crimson silks and adorned with all their jewels.
>
> "A small camel boy, perched in front of the throne, guides the beast and they ride backward and forward, on the actual edge of the battle, screaming encouragement to their warriors.
>
> "If a tribe goes down to absolute defeat, these chosen beauties become captive to the conquerors, but are treated with the greatest honor, and are even permitted to choose whom they will marry, though the most beautiful usually becomes a wife in the *hareem* of the sheik.
>
> "...... On the day of the battle between the Sirdieh (a small but daring tribe dwelling east of the Djebel Druse) and Annezy, Gutul rode with three other Sirdieh beauties, and kept screaming to the camel boy to push in closer. At a moment when the battle seemed to be going against her tribe, she leaned forward, seized the bamboo wand from the little camel boy's hand, then knocked him off his precarious perch, and drove the camel forward into the thick of the battle, crying at the top of her lungs the prolonged 'ooo!—ooo!— ooo!—ooo!' ...... with the other girls screeching and clawing at her in terror.
>
> "...... In the midst of the confusion and excitement, the Sirdieh rallied, and won the battle." (For this reference I am indebted to my friend and colleague, Dr. Sheldon H. Blank.)
>
> The author had this account only from a secondary source. It is rather vague in its details and probably should not be pressed too strongly. It seems to depict a modified tradition of the '*otfe*, in which the rôle of the battle maiden (cf. below) is emphasized at the expense of the original, independent rôle of the '*otfe* itself.

now the Roalla are the only Beduin in possession of one." If this last statement be correct, then it follows that by the end of the first decade of the 20th century, the other ʿoṭfe of which Lady Blunt and Rogers spoke as existent in their day, had disappeared, and only this one ʿoṭfe of the Ruwala was left. It is noteworthy too that Leachman speaks of it, just as did Musil at about the same time, as the *merkab*. Neither of them apparently heard it called ʿoṭfe, as the majority of the writers who preceded them did. The latter seems to have been the older and more specific name of this peculiar object, and of the entire class to which it belonged. *Merkab*, "vehicle," seems to be a younger and more general term for this class of objects.

That a young maiden of the tribe was usually the occupant of the ʿoṭfe, just as Wetzstein, Blunt, Rogers and Leachman, state, is clear from something further which Musil has to say.[123] "The Šḫûr lost their banner, el-bêraḳ, in an unsuccessful battle with Ibn Šaʿlân. It was borne by the ʿAṭfa'. ʿAṭfa' means a fully matured maiden who, adorned with her best ornaments, sits upon a good riding-camel, swings the banner and with words and lashes drives the animal into the midst of the enemy. She is surrounded by the chosen men of her tribe, who must defend her; for should she be captured, the battle is lost and the tribe may never again carry with them either ʿAṭfa' or banner."

Here Musil represents the maiden as the bearer of the tribal banner, and seems to have no thought of her connection with the ʿoṭfe. In fact he seems to have no knowledge at all of the ʿoṭfe, and no doubt for this reason he failed to identify the *abu ẓḫûr al-markab* of the Ruwala with the ʿoṭfe, as did Wetzstein, Blunt and Leachman. None the less the fact that the maiden who bears the tribal banner is known as the ʿaṭfa' indicates that this tribal banner is probably a comparatively late development among the Bedouin tribes, and that it is primarily a substitute for the older ʿoṭfe, gradually falling into disuse and disappearing, as practically all our authorities agree.

[123] *Arabia Petraea*, III, 377.

It indicates also that a maiden, and not an old woman, a boy or a slave, as Burckhardt states, was the customary occupant of the old ʻoṭfe. Perhaps, too, it is not without significance that the banner of the Shûr had its own name, el-bêraḳ (literally, "lightning"), just as has the ʻoṭfe of the Ruwala, abu ẓhûr al-merkab.

Doughty, too, has a brief but important word about this maiden.[124] Speaking of the well-clad and highly adorned maidens of the Beny Sâlem, a sub-tribe of the Harb, he says, "It seemed that any one of them might have been an Atáfa (or Ateyfa)—she that from her saddle frame warbles the battle-note, with a passionate sweetness, which kindles the manly hearts of the young tribesmen (and the Aarab are full of a wild sensibility).—They see her, each one as his spouse, without the veil, and decked as in the day of her marriage!—The Atáfa is a sheykh's daughter; but, said Hàmed, she may be another mezʼûna: it were infamous to kill an Atáfa; yet when shots flee, her camel may fall or run furiously, and the maiden-standard is in peril." From this passage it is clear that the name ʻatáfa, the technical term for the maiden who plays this rôle, is related to the name ʻoṭfe, and that it has survived among the Harb-Bedouin even though the ʻoṭfe itself has apparently disappeared, and the maiden has become but an ordinary, even though gayly dressed and adorned, camel-rider, spurring on the young warriors of her tribe to supreme efforts in battle. It indicates that at one time the institution of the ʻoṭfe was more general among the Arabs than it is at present, and that it is indeed, as Blunt and Rogers say, gradually disappearing. This passage also confirms our previous conclusion that originally the regular occupant of the ʻoṭfe was a maiden, the battle-maiden of the tribe, and not, as Burckhardt states, an old woman, a boy or a slave. This last, if correct, is probably a degenerate form of the older custom.

Elsewhere [125] Doughty writes as follows, "I might sometimes see heaving and rolling above all heads of men and cattle

---

[124] *Arabia Deserta*, II, 304.
[125] *Ibid.*, I, 61.

in the midst of the journeying caravan, the naked frame and posts of the sacred *Maḥmal* camel which resembles a bedstead, and is after the fashion of the Beduish woman's camel-litter. It is clothed on high days with a glorious pall of green velvet, the prophet's colour, and the four posts are crowned with glancing knops of silver. I understand from grave elders of the religion, that this litter is the standard of the Haj, in the antique guise of Arabia, and yet remaining among the Beduw; wherein, at any general battle of tribes, there is mounted some beautiful damsel of the sheykhs' daughters, whose generous loud *Alleluias* for her people, in presence of their enemies, inflame her young kinsmen's hearts to leap in that martial dance to a multitude of deaths." The comparison which Doughty makes here between the *maḥmal* of the pilgrim-caravan to Mecca and the ancient Bedouin 'otfe is suggestive indeed and leads to significant conclusions.

The *maḥmal* is described by Lane as follows;[126] "It is a square skeleton-frame of wood, with a pyramidal top; and has a covering of black brocade, richly worked with inscriptions and ornamental embroidery in gold, in some parts upon a ground of green or red silk, and bordered with a fringe of silk, with tassels surmounted by silver balls. Its covering is not always made after the same pattern with regard to the decorations; but in every cover that I have seen, I have remarked, on the upper part of the front, a view of the Temple of Mekkeh, worked in gold; and, over it, the Sultán's cypher. It contains nothing; but has two mus-hafs (or copies of the Kur-án), one on a scroll, and the other in the usual form of a little book, and each enclosed in a case of gilt silver, attached, externally, at the top... The five balls with crescents, which ornament the Mahmal, are of gilt silver. The Mahmal is borne by a fine tall camel, which is generally indulged with exemption from every kind of labour during the remainder of its life.

[126] *An Account of the Manners and Customs of the Modern Egyptians* (3rd ed.), 404 f.

"It is related that the Sultán Ez-Záhir Beybars, King of Egypt, was the first who sent a Mahmal with the caravan of pilgrims to Mekkeh, in the year of the Flight 670 (A. D. 1272), or 675; but this custom, it is generally said, had its origin a few years before his accession to the throne. Sheger-ed-Durr (commonly called Shegeret-ed-Durr), a beautiful Turkish female slave, who became the favourite wife of the Sultán Es-Sáleh Negm-ed-Deen, and on the death of his son (with whom terminated the dynasty of the house of Eiyoob) caused herself to be acknowledged as Queen of Egypt, performed the pilgrimage in a magnificent 'hódag' (or covered litter), borne by a camel; and for several successive years her empty hódag was sent with the caravan merely for the sake of state. Hence, succeeding princes of Egypt sent, with each year's caravan of pilgrims, a kind of hódag (which received the name of 'Mahmal' or 'Mahmil'), as an emblem of royalty; and the kings of other countries followed their example. The Wahhábees prohibited the Mahmal as an object of vain pomp; it afforded them one reason for intercepting the caravan."

This is the description of the Egyptian *maḥmal*. It is clear that Lane has given here, and in authoritative manner, the traditional account of the origin of this peculiar institution current in Cairo in the 19th century. According to this tradition the institution of the *maḥmal* is only approximately six hundred and fifty years old. The authenticity of this tradition is strongly questioned by Snouck Hurgronje,[127] who points out that in addition to this *maḥmal* from Cairo, and likewise the one from Damascus, to which Doughty refers, there were in ancient times various other *maḥmals*, representing the various parts and lands of the Moslem world and the princes who ruled over them. The *maḥmal* from Irak played an important rôle in the history of Mecca in 1320, but forty-nine years after the traditional date of the origin of the Egyptian *maḥmal*, and the *maḥmal* from Yemen played a similar rôle in 1380; and, as Snouck Hurgronje remarks, this was certainly not the first time that the latter *maḥmal* had

[127] *Mekka*, I, 84 ff.

come to Mecca. In the light of these facts he asks very pertinently how it is possible that all the rival princes of Moslem states should have hit upon exactly the same method of representing themselves in the pilgrimage to Mecca, so very soon after the custom had been instituted by the Egyptian princess. He is therefore inclined to believe that the institution of the *maḥmal* must have had some different and more ancient origin. He furthermore cites De Goeje,[128] who suggests the possibility of some relation between the *'otfe*, the *maḥmal* and the old Arabic custom of carrying portable shrines upon a journey or into battle. But these portable shrines can scarcely be aught other than the *'otfe* of the present-day Bedouin. Snouck Hurgronje likewise cites the custom still observed in Djiddah, the sea-port of Mecca, that in the celebration of their folk-festivals the people of the different quarters of the city make *maḥmals*, each quarter having its own festival and each its own *maḥmal*, and each trying to outdo its rival quarters in the fabrication of its *maḥmal*. These facts are significant. They point to the conclusion that the folk-tradition of the origin of the *maḥmal*, cited by Lane, is altogether unauthentic, and evidences no more than that the institution is of such antiquity that its true origin is entirely unknown to the modern Muslim.

Moreover, the facts cited by Lane, that no matter how the details of the external adornment of the Egyptian *maḥmal* may vary from year to year, two details are constant, viz. the representations of the Ka'aba, or the Temple at Mecca, and of the two copies of the Koran upon the front side

---

[128] *Mémoires d'histoire et de géographie orientales*,[2] No. 1, 180. De Goeje cites in particular the portable shrine of Mokhtar, mentioned by Tabari (translation Zotenberg, II, 702, 706). Unfortunately this is not accessible to me. However the same object was referred to by Ibn al-Wardy as follows; " In the year 66 of the Hejra, al-Mukhtar ibn 'Ubaid-Allâh ath-thaky went to al-Kûfa to avenge the blood of al-Hussein ... The al-Mukhtar took unto himself a throne (Kuray [this is probably an error for Kursay]), and proclaimed that it contained a mystery, being to them exactly what the ark was to the children of Israel, and when al-Mukhtar sent the army to attack 'Ubaid-Allah ibn Zayâd, he went out with this throne on a mule, which carried him (or it [undoubtedly the latter]) into battle." (Quoted from Rogers, *op. cit.*)

of the *maḥmal*-cover, coupled with the additional fact that, despite the Egyptian tradition that Sheger-ed-Durr occupied the first *maḥmal*, none the less all *maḥmals* are entirely empty, point to one significant conclusion, viz. that originally the *maḥmal*, whatever its earliest name among the Arabs may have been, was the empty litter in which the deity of the tribe or tribes to which it belonged, was thought to ride, while upon the many wanderings of the nomad tribe. Nay more, since the *maḥmal* in the present day appears only in the annual pilgrimage to Mecca, a difficult and dangerous journey indeed, particularly in ancient, and in fact until quite recent times, the thought suggests itself that originally the *maḥmal* was believed to be the actual guide of the pilgrim-caravan through the difficult and dangerous desert; it was thought to be the divine power which selected the road which the caravan must take, in order to arrive in safety at its destination. The peculiar, sacred character of the camel which bears the *maḥmal* tends to confirm this hypothesis. And perhaps some slight additional confirmation thereof may even be found in the tradition that it was a woman and a princess at that, who was the first occupant of the Egyptian *maḥmal*; for, as we have seen, the regular occupant of the *'otfe* was a maiden, and always the noblest maiden of the tribe. Unquestionably there is much probability to De Goeje's proposed correlation of the *maḥmal* and the *otfe*.

This conclusion is confirmed by certain additional considerations all pointing to the original conception of the *maḥmal* as being of divine character, or at least as possessing divine powers. Lane tells also,[129] in his description of the ceremonies incidental to the return of the *maḥmal* to Cairo, how he joined in the procession and came close to the *maḥmal*. "After touching it three times, and kissing my hand, I caught hold of the fringe, and walked by its side. The guardian of the sacred object, who walked behind it, looked very hard at me, and induced me to utter a pious ejaculation, which perhaps prevented his displacing me; or possibly my dress in-

---

[129] *Op. cit.*, 406 f.

fluenced him; for he only allowed other persons to approach and touch it one by one; and then drove them back. I continued to walk by its side, holding the fringe, nearly to the entrance of the Rumeyleh. On my telling a Muslim friend, to-day, that I had done this, he expressed great astonishment; and said that he had never heard of any one having done so before; and that the Prophet had certainly taken a love for me, or I could not have been allowed: he added, that I had derived an inestimable blessing; and that it would be prudent in me not to tell any others of my Muslim friends of this fact, as it would make them envy me so great a privilege, and perhaps displease them. I can not learn why the Mahmal is esteemed so sacred. Many persons showed an enthusiastic eagerness to touch it; and I heard a soldier exclaim, as it passed him, 'O my Lord! Thou hast denied my performing the pilgrimage!'"

From this account it is not clear whether the soldier's words, "O my Lord!", were addressed to the *maḥmal*, or were merely an ejaculation. But from the remainder of the account it is evident that a large measure of sanctity is popularly believed to reside in the *maḥmal*, and that he who merely touches or kisses it derives by contact a *baraka* or blessing, a portion of its sacred strength or power; therefore the sacred and taboo character of the camel which carried it upon the journey to and from Meccah and its exemption from work for the remainder of its life. For this reason too the fact that Lane was not only privileged to touch it just once, but to hold fast to the fringe and march alongside of the *maḥmal* for a considerable distance, implied that a very large measure of *baraka* had been permitted to pass into him. Of this fact, and also of the additional fact that he, a non-Moslem, had dared to touch the sacred object, his pious Moslem acquaintances may well have been jealous.

Lane's description of the *maḥmal* is corroborated in every detail by that of Rogers,[130] who likewise witnessed the procession incidental to its return from Meccah in 1882 or 1883.

---

[130] *Op. cit.*

He writes, "It is a large frame of wood, capable of being carried by a strong camel. When in the procession it is covered with a green veil, richly embroidered with ornaments and inscriptions in gold thread, and with heavy fringes and tassels. It is surmounted by silver-gilt knobs at the top and four corners, and a copy of the Kurân in a silver-gilt case is suspended from the top. Lane states that in his time the covering was black; but certainly for many years past it has been green... The Mahmil contains nothing.

"If one asks the Muslims of Cairo what the Mahmil is intended to represent, they only say that it is in memory of the camel-saddle and canopy in which the Mamluke Queen of Egypt, Shajar ad durr, performed her pilgrimage to Mekka and Medinah in the thirteenth century of our era. On asking whether such a ceremony existed before her time, they reply that they have no records of any previous Mahmil. I have frequently tried to elicit an expression of opinion as to some other origin, but without result. If the Mahmil be simply an emblem of the saddle on which a Queen of Egypt performed her pilgrimage, herself a foreigner and probably a convert to Islamism, not born in the faith, why should the Muslim world venerate it to such an extent? And, again, why does a similar Mahmil start simultaneously from Damascus?"

These questions are indeed apposite. They are practically the same as those raised by Snouck Hurgronje. They find a ready and natural answer in the proposed correlation of the *maḥmal* and the *'otfe*. And in fact Rogers himself, although, it must be admitted, upon rather superficial grounds and without any real understanding of the full implication of his hypothesis, suggested that there must have been an original relationship, a development from a common source, not only of the *maḥmal* and the *'otfe*, but also of the ancient ark of Israel.

From all this evidence it is clear that the *'otfe* is indeed an ancient institution among the Arabs, that in olden days it was much more common than it is to-day, and that, as a number of the authorities, whom we have cited, have remarked, the institution is gradually disappearing from among the Bedouin tribes, and in fact actually survives to-day in only a comparatively few tribes, and in these in what is probably a more or less degenerate form. The reason for this gradual disappearance of the ʿoṭfe is certainly not, as we have already remarked, that which Lady Blunt surmised, viz. the present-day difficulty of obtaining ostrich feathers with which to keep the ʿoṭfes in proper repair; for ostriches are hardly less plentiful to-day in the Arabian Desert than in ancient times, and had ostrich feathers been essential to the making and functioning of the ʿoṭfe, they would unquestionably have been used as generally in ancient days in the making of ʿoṭfes as they seem to be to-day; but this conclusion what little evidence there is does not support. Moreover, the maḥmal, apparently a variant and highly decorated form of the ʿoṭfe, has not the slightest suggestion of ostrich feathers in its makeup. Unquestionably the reason for the gradual disappearance of the ʿoṭfe from among the Bedouin tribes, given by Rogers, viz. the eventual capture and total destruction of almost all the tribal ʿoṭfes by hostile tribes, and the consequent inability of the original possessors of these captured ʿoṭfes to replace them, accounts for this circumstance far better.

Undoubtedly too this condition is furthered by a certain development and progress in Bedouin culture, extremely slow and almost imperceptible, it is true, but none the less real. This, coupled with the influence of Islam upon the life and practice of the Bedouin tribes, must have contributed not a little to the gradual disappearance of the ʿoṭfe. For while it is true that among these tribes the recognition and observance of Islam are more formal and superficial than real, this is true rather of the positive aspects of its observance than of the negative. Negatively Islam has exerted quite a far-reaching influence upon the old nomad life and institutions, in that, partly directly and officially and partly indirectly and unofficially, it has stamped certain ancient beliefs, rites and institutions as out of accord with fundamental Moslem principles, and has thus made for their gradual cessation and disappearance. This procedure is clearly illustrated by the Wahhaby attitude of disapproval of and opposition to the maḥmal, recorded by Snouck Hurgronje. Not improbably these Wahhaby rigorists have a suspicion, and perhaps even a faint knowledge, of a non-Islamic origin of the *maḥmal*, remote though this be. This process, which might be illustrated further by the history of the development of every religion, and not least of all by that of ancient Israel, and particularly by the Deuteronomic and early post-Deuteronomic attitude toward the ark, as we have established it, is the most natural and logical reason for the gradual disappearance of the ʿoṭfe.

Now it is significant that, with the single exception of the tradition of Shegger-ed-Durr, and this tradition has little or no historic evidence to validate it, the *maḥmal* always is empty, so far as human occupants are concerned. It is true that, according to Snouck Hurgronje, the various *maḥmal*s have appeared at Mecca in historical times, i. e. during the last six hundred and fifty years, as the representatives of the rulers of the chief lands or divisions of the Moslem world; but this is undoubtedly a secondary association, a concession to Islam and a modification of the original, non-Islamic import of the *maḥmal*. Still further concessions to Islam in this connection may be seen, perhaps, in the representation of the temple at Mecca upon the forward face of the cover of the Cairo *maḥmal*, and certainly in the fixing of a copy of the Koran, according to Rogers, or even two copies, one in scroll form and one in book form, according to Lane, on the upper part thereof. This association of *maḥmal* and Koran gave to the former an Islamic association and symbolism which unquestionably it did not possess originally. It assigned a definite and important place in the official worship of Allah to an institution which originally probably had little or no connection with the worship of this deity, unless perhaps in the "days of ignorance" before Mohammed, when it was in all likelihood one of the various, common, tribal symbols of pre-Islamic Arabian deities.

What its particular character and functions may have been in this early period, we can, of course, not determine, except to assume that they were the same as those of all other objects of this class, viz. to give victory to the tribesmen in battle and to guide the tribe upon its journeys through the desert.

A faint trace of this last function seems to have survived in the association of the maḥmal with the pilgrimage to Mecca and the attendant journey thither through the desert. But whether this points to a regular gathering at Meccah in pre-Islamic days of the maḥmals or ʿotfes or merkabs, or whatever may have been the official name of these peculiar objects in that remote period, for the celebration of a great, annual festival at the sanctuary there, it is, of course, scarcely possible to determine with certainty. Such a conclusion would, however, be quite probable in case such a festival had more than local significance, and served as the occasion for the gathering of many tribes for purposes of religious celebration. Then what more natural and probable than that each tribe should bring with it, and indeed feel that it had been led thither through the desert, by the symbol of its tribal deity? In the celebration of such a festival there would then have been a considerable gathering at Mecca of ʿotfes, maḥmals, merkabs, and other similar tribal palladia and symbols of tribal deities, such as actually took place there in connection with the celebration of the Hajj in the 13th and 14th centuries A.D. and likewise takes place, although to a much less extent, even in the present day.

Now, as has been said, with the single exception of Shegger-ed-Durr, there is no indication of the presence of a human occupant within the maḥmal, nor of the association of any human being with it in any kindred capacity. Nor is there any indication of or room for the presence of a human being, whether maiden or some other person, in the ʿotfe while on the march, and particularly while discharging the function of leading the tribe through the desert. The human being, whether maiden or old woman, slave or young boy, was present in the ʿotfe only when the latter went into battle, but apparently at no other time. And, as we have seen, participation in battle seems to be, or to have been, but one of the important functions of the ʿotfe. The presumption is strong therefore that the presence of a human being in the ʿotfe, even during a battle, is not original and primary, but that it is rather secondary, and probably the result of the fusion of two ancient institutions, both of which apparently underwent considerable modification in the course of time, chiefly because of the growing influence of Islam, and both of which even threatened to disappear completely, as they are, in fact, doing to-day. Such a condition and such an impending fate tend mightily to such fusion and to the consequent acquisition of renewed strength and power of perpetuation for a time of the newly organized institution resulting from the fusion. This fusion, if this assumption be correct, must itself have been of considerable antiquity, as the not inconsiderable mass of evidence thereof, and particularly the development of the technical name, 'atâfa or 'ateyfa, recorded by Doughty, indicates.

This institution of the battle-maiden in the practice of warfare among Semitic tribes seems to be of great antiquity, even though the evidence therefor, due to easily comprehensible reasons, is scanty indeed. In addition to the general evidence of the practice among Bedouin tribes, not only in modern, but likewise in ancient days, we have the specific instance of Aisha playing just this rôle at the Battle of the Camel in the year 36 A.H. (656 A.D.).[131] In this battle Aisha rode upon a thoroughbred camel, of unusual value. She was in the thick of the battle, spurring on her warriors to heroic efforts. Seventy men of the Banū Ḍabba fell about her in the vain attempt to defend her. Her camel was killed in the battle and she was captured by Ali. She was treated by him with every possible consideration and given her complete freedom.[132] We do not know that the term 'atâfa was actually applied to Aisha in connection with her rôle in this battle, nor that the camel upon which she rode was caparisoned with an actual 'otfe. But certainly she did play exactly the rôle of the battle maiden on this occasion; and apparently it was not a novel nor unfamiliar rôle to her or her contemporaries and was governed by definite regulations and principles. It may be inferred too, from the charge to Deborah, in Jud. 5. 12, to recite her song in the battle of the Israelite tribes against their Canaanite foes, that in this battle she too played the rôle of

---

[131] So Hartmann, " Zelt und Lade," *ZAW*, 37 (1917–1918), 222.
[132] Cf. article, " Aisha," *Encyclopedia of Islam*, I, 216 f.

the battle-maiden, spurring the warriors of Israel to valorous deeds and to victory against their enemies.[133] But if so, then the institution of the battle-maiden must have existed also in ancient Israel.

We can readily understand why this institution should have disappeared regularly at a fairly early stage of the cultural evolution of Semitic peoples and have left but little trace in their literatures. For it is self-apparent that this institution is intimately bound up with and adapted only to early, tribal methods of warfare. So soon as Semitic peoples advanced beyond primitive tribal organization and form of government and methods of warfare, and developed an intertribal, and eventual monarchical, system of government and new methods of systematic warfare by well-organized and disciplined armies, the old institution of the battle-maiden was bound to disappear. And since this phase of cultural evolution as a rule went hand in hand with, or perhaps even preceded somewhat, the development of the art of writing and the free production of literature, it follows naturally that in Semitic literature references to the institution of the battle-maiden are comparatively few and obscure. But the evidence which we have gathered, scanty though it undoubtedly is, suffices to establish as probable that in the primitive days of Semitic tribal life and warfare the institution was fairly common, if not quite general. But the evidence also seems to indicate that it was originally an altogether independent institution, which had no primary association of any kind with the ʻotfe or other objects of this class, and that the present connection is due entirely, as we have suggested, to

---

[133] If this assumption be correct, then in both cases of Aisha and Deborah, this rôle was played, not by a maiden, but by a woman well along in years. For Aisha was forty-three years old at the time of the Battle of the Camel; and to have built up the reputation and influence among the tribes which she apparently enjoyed at the time of the Battle of Taanach, Deborah too must have been a woman well advanced in age. This agrees with the statement of Burckhardt that an old woman frequently played the rôle of occupant of the ʻotfe and of battle-maiden. Certainly both Deborah and Aisha were women of highest standing and influence, not only in their own, but even among neighboring and kindred tribes.

the common fate of being outgrown culturally and eventually disappearing, which impended over both, which tended among the Bedouin tribes to fuse them and give them some renewed strength and power of persistence for a time.[134] But if this inference be correct, it would follow further that originally the ʿotfe or its historic antecedent was always empty, even when going into battle, precisely as the maḥmal is to-day and the ʿotfe or merkab itself also on all occasions except in battle.

Returning now to the ʿotfe, it is clear that the account given by Musil is surprising indeed. For it differs in quite a number of significant details from the specific descriptions of the very same object by Wetzstein and Lady Blunt. There can be no question as to the reliability of Musil's testimony; for on the one hand, he is too careful and authoritative an observer and master of Bedouin life and custom, and too experienced an investigator thereof, to have been misled; and on the other hand, the information given him about the *abu ẓhûr al-markab* agrees too completely with the facts which we have been able to establish concerning the early form and functions of the forerunners of the present-day ʿotfe and maḥmal, to be questioned. It is of course strange, and in fact almost inexplicable, that the information which Musil should have been able to gather from the Ruwala about the *abu ẓhûr al-markab*, from thirty to forty years after both Wetzstein and the Blunts had visited the same tribe, is so different and so much more primitive in certain essential details; but even such a condition is not impossible nor does it give any reason for questioning the correctness of Musil's statement, particularly since it is corroborated by the entirely independent testimony of Curtiss with regard to the significant fact of the name *abu ẓhûr* or Abu ed-Duhûr.

At any rate Musil's description of this strange object, in contrast to the other accounts which we have quoted, emphasizes the most primitive features of its character and

---

[134] It is perhaps of some significance in this connection that Musil heard nothing at all, apparently, of the maiden in connection with the *abu ẓhûr al-markab*, although both Wetzstein and the Blunts heard of her explicitly in just this connection.

functions. It determines the way through the desert which the tribe must go; it gives the tribe victory in battle; a deity, whether Allah, as Musil was told, or Abu ed-Duhûr, as the name implies, dwells in it, and imparts his will, and thus gives indication of future events, either by the fluttering of the ostrich feathers upon the object, even though there be no wind at the time, or by the object inclining itself to one side; every year a white camel is sacrificed before this object, i. e. of course to the deity resident in or associated with it, and the blood of this sacrifice is sprinkled upon the corner posts thereof.[135] This is primitive Semitic concept and practice indeed.

But just this description, in almost every detail, applies to the ark of Israel also. It too, according to Biblical tradition, selected the road which Israel was to travel through the desert; it too gave victory in battle; in it too a deity apparently was thought to dwell, and from it to give oracular decisions. And while there is no explicit evidence that in the earliest period of its history sacrifices were actually offered directly to the ark or to the deity thought to dwell in it, and that the blood thereof was sprinkled upon the ark, due entirely to the paucity of the evidence bearing upon the ark coming from this earliest period, it would be altogether reasonable to assume that such sacrifices were actually offered.[136] And

[135] Inasmuch as Abu ed-Duhûr seems to be, according to Curtiss, a kind of ancestral deity of the Ruwala, and inasmuch also as the *abu ẓhûr al-markab* goes into battle and brings victory to the tribe, this sacrifice may be regarded, in part at least, as offered originally to the tribal ancestral deity who gives victory in battle. It may therefore be compared with the sacrifice which the 'aḳîd, or tribal military leader, offers in the evening preceding an anticipated battle, with the words, "This is thy supper, O our ancestor; help us today!, *hâḏa 'ašâk jâ ǧiddina tufze' lana-l-jowm.*" (Musil, *Arabia Petraea*, III, 382.)

[136] Not improbably the sacrifices recorded in I Sam. 6. 14 and II Sam. 6. 13, 17 were just such sacrifices, offered directly to the ark, and with the blood even sprinkled upon the ark, although the present text, accommodated to later theology, states explicitly that these sacrifices were offered to Yahwe, or " before Yahwe," literally " into the face of Yahwe." For this last expression as a technical term in the sacrificial parlance of modern Palestine, cf. Curtiss, *Primitive Semitic Religion Today*, English edition, Chap. XVI; German edition, Chap. 22.

this assumption would find strong confirmation in the practice recorded in the Priestly Code, of offering sacrifices before the holy of holies in which the ark was supposed to stand, and of sprinkling the blood thereof upon the veil before the ark, towards Yahwe, i. e. towards the ark itself,[137] and, in the particularly solemn ceremonies of the Day of Atonement, the ancient New Year's Day, even upon the *kapporet* itself,[138] the empty golden throne of Yahwe resting, according to Priestly tradition, on top of the ark. Unquestionably at the bottom of this last ceremony lies some ancient New Year's Day rite, the origin of which may well reach back to that early period of Israel's history when sacrifice was actually offered directly to the ark, or to the deity thought to dwell within it, and the blood thereof was sprinkled upon the top or the four corners of the ark. This ceremony would then be practically identical with that practiced to-day by the Ruwala upon the *abu ẓhûr al-markab*. In the light of these facts there can not be the slightest question that the ancient ark of Israel was originally an object of the same kind and class as the *'otfe* and the *maḥmal*[139] of the present-day Arabs, and particularly of the *abu ẓhûr al-markab*[140] of the Ruwala.

We have seen that a deity was thought to dwell within the ark. The question arises here whether the ark was empty

---

[137] Lev. 4. 6, 17.   [138] Lev. 16. 14 f.

[139] In this connection it is of considerable significance to note that the two copies of the Koran affixed to the upper part of the front face of the *maḥmal* parallel in both character and purpose the two tablets of the Decalogue which tradition located in the ark. Both Korans and stone tablets served to give to what was originally an idolatrous or semi-idolatrous cult-object a sanction and a definite, legitimate place in the comparatively advanced worship of the new national deities, Yahwe in the religion of Israel and Allah in Islam. But why *two* stone tablets and *two* copies of the Koran it is difficult to determine. (Cf. note 149.) But the coincidence in the number two is probably not without significance.

[140] Torczyner (" Die Bundeslade und die Anfänge der Religion Israels," *Festschrift zum 50 jährigen Bestehen der Hochschule für die Wissenschaft des Judentums*, 264) correctly correlates the element *al-markab* in the name *abû ẓhûr al-markab* with, on the one hand, the early function of the ark as a מרכבה or means of transportation of the deity thought to dwell within, and המרכבה associated with the cherubim in I Chron. 28. 18, and, on the other hand, with the Rabbinical tradition which represented Ezekiel's picture of the $k^ebod\ Yahwe$ and its method of transportation as המרכבה.

of any concrete object, or whether there was actually something within the ark with which the presence of this deity was associated. The question is difficult indeed, and in fact, because of lack of direct evidence no final and positive answer can be given to it.

One thing seems almost certain, that if the ark did contain some concrete object, this was certainly not an image, as Gressmann claims.[141] For the presence of an image or idol or any object of specific shape, would imply its exhibition on particular occasions; and there is not the slightest evidence of any such procedure in connection with the ark in any of the periods of its history. Instead the constant implication is that the deity is always within, and never outside the ark, as the presence of any image or like object fashioned in some particular shape for occasional display, would imply.

Furthermore, on first glance it seems that the ark might well be compared to those vehicles, whether boats or wagons or palanquins, borne by human beings or animals, in which the images of Babylonian and Egyptian deities were carried during their festal processions. And indeed both Gunkel [142] and Gressmann [143] have made this comparison. Nor can it be denied that in the third period of its history, and even during the transition from the second to the third period, marked by Ezekiel's conception of the enthroned *kebod Yahwe*, the ark did perform, in part at least, the functions of these vehicles of divine transportation. It is true, too, that the ark, likewise during the first period of its history, would seem to have resembled these vehicles, since it, too, was transported hither and thither, into battle or along the road through the desert, and of course in such journeyings, the deity associated with it invariably accompanied it. But this last comparison is more seeming than real. For both the Babylonian and Egyptian objects referred to were vehicles of transportation of the images of the gods and nothing more. They had no immediate and inseparable connection with the deity himself

[141] *Die Lade Jahves*, 17 ff.
[142] " Die Lade Jahves ein Thronsitz," *ZMR*, 1906.
[143] *Op. cit.*

or with the image or object by which he was represented. Only during the few, brief moments of physical transportation of the image in the procession was it in direct contact and association with this vehicle, and at all other times the vehicle had but little, and that only secondary, divine significance. But with the ark it was entirely different. Whatever the contents of the ark may have been, by which the deity was symbolized, or in which he was thought to dwell, it was never removed nor dissociated from the ark, nor was the ark ever opened that it might be exhibited to the public gaze. It remained constantly within the ark, inseparably associated with it, so completely and concretely that the ark itself came in popular thought and speech to be identified with the deity; the ark itself was to all intents and purposes the deity, and to lay unguarded and ritually unfit hand upon the ark was exactly the same in effect as to lay hand upon the sacred object within; it violated the taboo in which that particular deity was enwrapped and entailed death. Only incidentally, therefore, and not at all fundamentally, was the ark, during the first period of its history, in any way similar to these vehicles of sacred transportation of the Babylonian and Egyptian religions. Its relationship to the ʻotfe, particularly in the earliest stages of the development of this object, is manifestly far closer.

What then was the ark; or rather, and more correctly, what could the contents of the ark have been? The most natural assumption is that the ark contained a *betyl* or sacred stone.[144] This conception was, of course, common among the primitive Semites,[145] and the evidence is ample that it was current in ancient Israel, particularly among the northern tribes.[146] This was the most natural and likely object in which

[144] So also Stade, *Geschichte des Volkes Israel*, I, 457 f.; Benzinger, *Hebräische Archäologie*,¹ 369; Bertholet, *Kulturgeschichte Israels*, 99.

[145] Cf. Robertson Smith, *The Religion of the Semites*,² 200 ff.

[146] Cf. Gen. 28. 20–22, and the name of the sanctuary and city Bethel. Ex. 3. 2 ff. records a tradition of undoubtedly great antiquity, that Yahwe dwelt originally in the סְנֶה (notice הַסְּנֶה, always with the article, i. e. therefore, *the* סנה, the well-known סנה, well-known, of course, just because Yahwe was thought to dwell in it) upon Mount Horeb in the desert. Since this tradition is found in

a deity who must move or be transported from place to place would be thought to dwell. Such powers could scarcely be ascribed to a primitive deity thought to sojourn in a sacred tree or spring. Such deities are of necessity inseparably bound to one fixed spot, and at that spot they must remain forever localized until eventually their worship is outgrown and the memory of them disappears. But a deity thought to dwell in a sacred stone can well be conceived of as moving or being moved from place to place; and just such a deity was the god of the ark.

Moreover, the dominant tradition of the second period of the history of the ark, as we have seen, was that it contained two sacred stones, sacred it is true, not because a deity was thought to dwell in them, but only because the divinely revealed Decalogue was thought to be inscribed upon them; but sacred none the less. It is true that this tradition might have developed entirely independently of the presence in the original ark of a sacred stone. But, as we have suggested, in all likelihood the tradition of the two tablets of the Decalogue in the ark is secondary, and in its original form the tradition told only of the scroll of the Book of the Covenant within the ark. It would have been far more natural for the tradition to have retained this, its original form, since writing upon a scroll was more simple and general than engraving upon stone tablets.[147] In all likelihood therefore there was some good

the Elohist Code, it is probably of northern, Israelite origin. On first thought, therefore, it would be natural to correlate this tradition with the Ephraimite tradition of the ark and its deity, and to assume that what was in the ark was either this מצבה itself or a piece thereof. This would not be at all impossible. But it is hardly probable, since to remove the מצבה from the spot where it originally stood would have destroyed its life, and would no doubt have thereby terminated automatically whatever attributes of divinity this מצבה was thought to have possessed.

[147] Even upon the famous relief upon the Hammurapi-stone, Shamash, the sun-god, seems to be handing to the king a copy of the laws inscribed upon a scroll. It is difficult to conceive of the object in the sun-god's right hand, outstretched to the king, as aught else. This is all the more noteworthy since just in Babylonia writing upon scrolls was far less common than upon clay bricks, and since, furthermore, this law code of Hammurapi, at least in the copy that has come down to us, was inscribed not upon a scroll but upon a stone monument.

reason for the development of this secondary and less natural form of the tradition, viz. that of the two stone tablets. And the simplest and most probable reason, and in fact the only one that can possibly be conceived of, is that early fact or tradition did know of the presence of a sacred stone in the ark, and that a strong remembrance of this persisted into the second period of the history of the ark. Consequently even after the attempt had been made to supplant the old fact or tradition by the new tradition that the ark contained the scroll of the Book of the Covenant, this new tradition was in time accommodated to the original tradition and so modified as to tell now that the ark did actually contain a sacred stone, or rather two sacred stones, but sacred now, no longer because a deity was thought to dwell in them, but only because the Decalogue was inscribed upon them.[148] In such case the

[148] In this connection it is perhaps of some significance that the form of this tradition apparently current in the Northern Kingdom, since it is recorded in E (Ex. 32. 16), ascribed a larger and more directly divine character to the tablets of the Decalogue than did the form of the tradition apparently current in the Southern Kingdom, since it is recorded in J (Ex. 34. 1 ff.). E told that not only had the Deity revealed the Decalogue to Moses, but He had likewise prepared the tablets and inscribed the ten " words " upon them with His own hands. On the other hand, J told that it was Moses who prepared the tablets, although at Yahwe's command, and that he brought them with him up the mountain, and that Yahwe merely inscribed the Decalogue upon them. It is noteworthy too that D (Deut. 10. 1-4) follows J rather than E in this tradition. This is all the more significant, since ordinarily D follows E in preference to J. This seems to accord with the fact already noted, that the D writers held the ark and its contents in less esteem than did an earlier age and its writers. Perhaps for this reason they placed the stamp of their approval upon the J tradition, because it ascribed somewhat less of sanctity to the two tablets than did the E tradition.

We have already seen that the oldest traditions, those of K and C, knew nothing of the divine character of their scrolls of the " words," but told simply and naturally that Moses wrote these " words " upon a scroll.

In this connection, and for the sake of completeness, mention must be made of the hypothesis that the ark was naught other than the coffin of Joseph in which his bones or mummy were deposited. This hypothesis has been suggested more or less hesitatingly by Loisy, *The Religion of Israel*, 91; Volter, *Ägypten und die Bibel*, 92 f.; Hartmann, " Zelt und Lade," *ZAW*, XXXVII (1917–1918), 237. According to Biblical and rabbinic tradition the coffin of Joseph was carried by Israel upon the exodus and the journey through the

tradition of the two sacred stone tablets within the ark would point strongly to the conclusion that the original contents of the ark must have been a sacred stone.[149] But since, as we have seen, a deity was thought to dwell within the ark, such a sacred stone within the ark could have been only a betyl, a stone in which a deity was thought to dwell, and naught else.

However, the question of what the ark actually contained is really, because of the insufficiency of the evidence and the uncertainty of the conclusions which may be drawn from them, of secondary importance. The outstanding and indubitable fact is that the ark was thought to contain something, and this something, whatever it was, was either conceived of as the deity himself, or as the object in which the deity was thought to reside permanently. Because of this the ark itself was very naturally identified with the deity thought to dwell in it, and was regarded therefore as an inherently sacred object, endowed with all the qualities of divine function and taboo.

Moreover, the ark was intimately, and apparently, inseparably associated with Shiloh. There was the sanctuary in which the ark stood, and there it, or rather the deity associated with it, was ministered to by the Levitical priestly family of Eli. From this sanctuary at Shiloh the ark was brought down to battle against the Philistines at Eben Haezer. And inasmuch as Shiloh lay in the territory of Ephraim, and was, as I Sam. 1 clearly indicates, the center of worship of the tribe of Ephraim,

---

wilderness. It was believed too to possess miraculous powers, such as being able to move of its own accord and even to select the way which it wished to go (cf. *Jewish Encyclopedia*, VII, 251; Ginzberg, *The Legends of the Jews*, II, 181 ff.). But outside of these matters there are no significant points of contact between the ark and the coffin of Joseph. And as we have seen, such powers as these are commonly attributed in the Orient to the coffins] of saints. It is of course quite natural and probable that some of the details of this tradition were borrowed from the older tradition of the ark.

[149] Or perhaps two sacred stones. For an ingenious but hardly convincing explanation of the reason for two stones, cf. Torczyner, *op. cit.*, 252 f. On the other hand, Proksch (*Das Nordhebräische Sagenbuch — Die Elohim-Quelle*, 374) is inclined to believe that there were no stones at all in the ark.

to which all its members pilgrimed at least once a year to offer their sacrifices and fulfill their vows, it follows that the ark with its contents must have been primarily the cult object of Ephraim.[150] It must have played for this tribe precisely the same rôle which the stolen ephod of Micah played for the tribe of Dan,[151] which the ephod which Gideon set up at Ophrah did for Manasseh,[152] which apparently the ephod at Nob, which Ebiathar brought down with him to David, did for Benjamin,[153] and which presumably other similar objects did for the other northern tribes.[154] As the cult object of Ephraim it was the center of its tribal worship, and was the natural object to go into battle with its tribe and give them victory over their foes. As a tribal cult-object discharging these functions its close relationship to objects like the *abu ẓhûr al-markab* of the present-day Ruwala is doubly apparent.

In all likelihood, too, at the time of its capture by the Philistines, the ark had come to enjoy a considerable intertribal reputation, due to the position of influence and leadership among the northern tribes which Ephraim had acquired. Quite probably the sanctuary at Shiloh was frequented to a considerable extent by members of other kindred tribes belonging to that federation of central and northern tribes, in which Ephraim held the dominant position. In the two battles

---

[150] So also Wellhausen, *Prolegomena zur Geschichte Israels*[6] 45 f., note; Benzinger, *op. cit.*; Winckler, *Geschichte Israels*, I, 72, note 2; Bertholet, *op. cit.*, 100; Proksch, *op. cit.*

[151] Jud. 17–18.

[152] Jud. 8. 26 f.

[153] I Sam. 21. 10; 23. 6, 9.

[154] I have suggested elsewhere ("The Oldest Document of the Hexateuch," *HUCA*, IV [1927], 125, note 119) that the brazen serpent in the Temple at Jerusalem may have been originally a similar cult-object of some tribe, though of just which one it can no longer be determined, and that it was brought up to Jerusalem by David for much the same reason that he brought up the ark thither (cf. above, note 78). As we have likewise seen (*ibid.*, 119 ff.), the tribe of Judah, apparently alone of all the tribes, seems to have had no such cult-object or representation of a tribal deity whatsoever, but had instead originally its "tent of meeting," whither Yahwe was thought to come from His abode upon the sacred mountain in the desert, and there meet with the people, represented by the oracular priest.

of Eben Haezer, it was not merely Ephraim, but all the tribes belonging to this federation, whose warriors were present, and it was because of this common defeat of all these tribes on this occasion that not merely the territory of Ephraim, but that of other tribes as well, and particularly that of Manasseh, the tribe adjacent to and most closely related to Ephraim, was overrun as far north as the Valley of Jezreel and Beth-Shean on the Jordan, and conquered by the Philistines. This federation, which was probably more a loose and tacit association of neighboring tribes, than a definite and systematic organization, had sprung up largely as the result of the common danger faced and the common victory gained by the Israelite tribes over their Canaanite enemies at the Battle of Taanach. Dan apparently had held itself aloof from this federation,[155] and had therefore later to fight its battle alone and unaided against the aggressive Philistines. It was badly defeated in this war and lost much of its man-power. Finally, reduced to a mere six hundred fighting men, it found itself unable to remain in its first place of settlement in Palestine and was compelled to seek a new home far to the north.[156] Benjamin had undoubtedly been one of the tribes participating in the Battle of Taanach,[157] and therefore must have been originally a member of this federation. But it had apparently withdrawn therefrom as the result of civil strife, particularly with Ephraim,[158] and in consequence did not participate in the Battle of Eben Haezer. For this reason its strength remained unimpaired by the outcome of this battle and its territory unconquered by the Philistines. Therefore it was free and ready to take up the contest against the Philistines a half century later, when Samuel, the Ephraimite, succeeded in inspiring Saul the Benjamite with his own zeal for this cause.

But the tribes participating in the Battle of Eben Haezer, Ephraim, Manasseh, and probably also, although perhaps not to quite the same extent, since their danger was not so immediate, Issachar, Zebulon and Naphtali, must have looked upon the ark as their common palladium, and have confidently

[155] Jud. 5. 17. [156] Jud. 17–18. [157] Jud. 5. 14. [158] Jud. 19–21.

expected that its presence in battle would ensure them victory over their hated foes. Accordingly, it would seem, they did not hesitate to stake everything upon this one battle, the second Battle of Eben Haezer, in which the ark was present. Their defeat was overwhelming. These tribes were conquered and their spirits crushed. Their territory now became the prey of the triumphant Philistines. The ark was captured; and even though it did succeed in delivering itself from the Philistines, and did likewise preserve its reputation as a powerful deity and cult-object, never again did it return to its former abode in Shiloh. Eventually it found its way up to the national sanctuary at Jerusalem, where, as we have seen, it came gradually, naturally and inevitably to be conceived in a new light and as discharging a new function, altogether unrelated to those which it had originally been thought to discharge; and in time an altogether new tradition grew up about it. And perhaps, as we have suggested, one of the strong reasons for the lack of spirit and courage on the part of the northern tribes at the time of Saul's rebellion against the Philistines, and their failure to rally to this leader's support, as he had unquestionably expected, was just the absence of the ark, their old palladium and guarantee of victory, from their midst. Without it, they thought no doubt, victory was impossible. So long as the ark was not with them, the Philistine yoke could not be thrown off; rebellion was hopeless.

VI

The Deity of the Ark

One final question remains to be answered, viz. as to the deity of the ark. There is not the slightest evidence that this deity was ever aught other than Yahwe. The name of no other deity is mentioned in connection with the ark, nor is there the slightest indication of the relationship of any other deity to it. But it is important to realize that all our evidence bearing upon the ark comes from the period following upon the settlement of the tribes of Israel in Palestine, and after an intertribal consciousness and sense of relationship had attained a considerable development. And with this, of course, went hand in hand the development of the concept of a deity who was more than tribal, who in fact enjoyed, as we have seen, a considerable intertribal regard and worship. With the single exception of the tradition of its leadership of Israel through the desert, our oldest evidence bearing upon the ark comes from near the close of the period of tribal settlement in Palestine, and antedates by but little more than a century the establishment of the nation by David. Therefore, even if Yahwe had not been the original deity of the ark, there had been ample time and opportunity for His worship to have spread among the northern tribes, and to have supplanted, in connection with the ark, the worship, and even the name, of the deity originally associated with it. An almost exact parallel would be found in the manner in which Allah has almost entirely supplanted the original Abu ed-Duhûr of the Ruwala 'otfe; and the tradition was communicated to Musil that Allah sometimes takes his seat in this 'otfe. Only the name, *abû ẓhûr* has survived, and this apparently in a form changed somewhat from its original sound, and with a popular, new, artificial, etymological explanation of the name.

It is, needless to say, not at all impossible that a similar process may have taken place with the ark; that originally, some deity other than Yahwe, of course the eponymous, ancestral deity of the tribe of Ephraim, may have been associated with it, but that, by the comparatively advanced historical period from which our oldest evidence dates, his association and his worship and even his name had been so completely supplanted by those of Yahwe, the developing intertribal deity, that not even the slightest remininscence thereof survived, and in consequence we find in all our evidence only the name Yahwe associated with the ark. The fact that at this moment when the ark first appears upon the stage of history, a priestly family of unquestionably Levitical lineage,[159] and therefore

---

[159] Cf. Meyer, *Die Israeliten und ihre Nachbarstämme*, 451.

devoted champions of Yahwe, is ministering to it, might account to a large extent for the supplanting of such an original deity of the ark by Yahwe.

But while such a hypothesis would be altogether natural and possible, and is undoubtedly even quite plausible, there is on the other hand not the slightest actual evidence in favor of it, or pointing to any conclusion other than that Yahwe was from the very beginning connected with the ark, was the deity thought to reside in it. This would mean, of course, that Yahwe was originally the tribal deity of Ephraim, just as, as we have seen,[160] He was originally the tribal deity of the Kenites, from whom His worship passed, by virtue of the covenant relation established between Him and them, to the southern tribes of Judah, Simon and Levi. But this does not mean at all that the original Yahwe of Ephraim was necessarily the same as the Yahwe of the Kenites. We have seen that the latter was strictly a local deity, intimately and inseparably associated with the mountain in the desert, called therefore in the Kenite document, "the mountain of Yahwe." Not improbably Yahwe was not altogether the proper name of one particular deity. It may well have been at this time the common designation for quite a considerable number of local, tribal or clan deities of this particular class, deities associated with various spots out in the desert, worshiped by different desert clans or tribes, and thought to bestow upon them satisfaction of the basic needs and blessings of nomad life. Such a class of desert, pastoral deities would, of course, differ radically and contrast significantly with the Canaanite, agricultural Be'alim, when once they came into direct contact, after the tribes of Israel had begun to force their way into Palestine Perhaps in such an assumption of many local and tribal Yahwes we find the best and most natural explanation of the otherwise difficult problem of the parallel names of and traditions about the two sacred mountains in the desert, Sinai and Horeb, as well as the "mountain of Yahwe" of K. Certainly Sinai and Horeb were not originally merely two dif-

---

[160] "The Oldest Document, &c.," *HUCA*, IV [1927], 101 f.

ferent names for one and the same mountain. The conflicting Biblical traditions with regard to the location of the mountain of revelation, as well as the presence of these two names, and the scrupulousness with which they are kept apart by the J and E writers, establish this conclusion. Not impossibly either Sinai or Horeb may be identified with "the moutain of Yahwe" of K, although this is by no means certain. We have accordingly authentic Biblical traditions of at least two, and possibly three, different, sacred mountains in the desert upon which a Yahwe was originally thought to dwell. And this fact may well point to at least two or three original tribal Yahwes, each associated with a different mountain in the desert, undoubtedly conceived of as his original abode.

This entire argument is, it must be admitted, in the main hypothetical. And yet it has much in its favor. For, on the one hand, by whatever names the different tribes, which later, after their entrance into and settlement in Palestine, came to compose the federation, and ultimately the nation of Israel, called their respective tribal deities, it is certain that they conceived of all these deities in much the same manner and as discharging practically identical functions and bestowing upon their respective tribes much the same blessings of protection and pastoral abundance and numerous progeny. For just this reason it was easy for the tribes coming forth from Egypt, and convinced through bitter experience of the impotence of their old tribal deities, to adopt the worship of a new deity, who differed from their former tribal deities only in individuality and in the place where he was thought to dwell, and but little, if at all, in character, function and manner of worship. For the same reason, too, the tribe of Dan, likewise convinced through severe misfortune and tribal calamity of the powerlessness of its former tribal deity, could renounce his worship and in his place take a new deity, undoubtedly one of the same character and class as its former deity, but one presumably more powerful.[161]

---

[161] Jud. 17–18.

For such a group or class of desert, pastoral deities there must have been some general name or title to designate the class. This title may well have been Yahwe; and these different Yahwes may have been distinguished from each other, just as were the Beʿalim of Palestine, either by subordinate proper names, or, more likely, by coupling the name Yahwe either with the particular spot in the desert where he was thought to have his fixed abode, or with the name of the clan or tribe who were his original worshipers.[162] Thus we would have the Yahwe of Sinai, the Yahwe of Horeb,[163] the Yahwe of Ephraim, &c.

One additional consideration strengthens the probability of this hypothesis. If it be not correct, and there was instead only one original Yahwe and no more, then He could have been only the Yahwe of "the mountain of Yahwe" of the Kenite document, the Yahwe of the Kenites, whose worship passed from them to the group of tribes who came forth from Egypt and settled in southern Palestine, Judah, Simon and

---

[162] This last statement is to be understood only in the most general sense. For there is considerable evidence that the tribes of Israel, as we know them in historical times, were in large part a comparatively late development. When the Israelites entered Palestine *beena* marriage still flourished among them to a considerable extent; and under the conditions of *beena* marriage, with relationship traced through the mother and in the direction of the mother's brothers, the basic social unit was not the tribe but the clan, the *mišpaḥa*. Largely as one of the first effects of contact with superior Canaanite culture, *baʿal* marriage gradually supplanted *beena* marriage; and this fact was one of the chief contributing forces to the eventual development of the tribe as the basic social and political unit in Israel during the early sojourn in Palestine. This in turn brought about the reduction of the clan to a smaller compass and a position of less social and political importance, and the gradual fusion of various original clans, such as Machir, Abi-Ezer, Gilead and the like into new, larger and more powerful tribes, such as Manasseh and Gad. This question I shall discuss in detail elsewhere. But if the clan was the basic social unit in the pre-Canaanite days, then we should speak of clan gods rather than of tribal gods.

[163] The Yahwe of Horeb would, of course, have been likewise the Yahwe thought to reside in the סנה upon this mountain. This is a most typical and significant instance of the old, pre-Canaanite, desert, local Yahwes. For certainly this Yahwe of the סנה on Mount Horeb could not possibly have been identical with the Yahwe of the sacred mountain with the cave upon it of the K document.

Levi. And, in such case, only from them could the worship of Yahwe have passed to the northern tribes. But we shall see in time,[164] that this southern group of tribes were the very last to enter Palestine, and that their entrance preceded the Battle of Taanach by but a few years.[165] And already in the Song of Deborah we find Yahwe the only Israelite deity mentioned, and mentioned in such manner that there is scarcely room for the assumption that this name was substituted later for the names of other Israelite clan or tribal deities which originally stood there. And it is clear from this ancient Israelite poem that already at this time among these northern tribes Yahwe enjoyed a considerable intertribal reputation. It is futile therefore to suppose that the worship of Yahwe was not original with these northern tribes, and that it must have passed to them from the southern tribes, largely through the mediation of the Levites, playing the rôle of intertribal priests of Yahwe. It is true that the Levites did come at quite an early period, following very shortly upon their settlement in southern Palestine,[166] to play this rôle of intertribal priests of Yahwe. Actually, however, this rôle was facilitated by the fact that Yahwe had evolved quite far as an intertribal deity already when the Levites appeared upon the scene, rather than the reverse, that Yahwe, originally the tribal deity of the Kenites alone, came to be regarded as an intertribal deity largely through the mediation and propaganda of these Levitical priests.

Therefore, while it must be acknowledged that the evidence is altogether insufficient to warrant any absolute assertion, none the less the large preponderance of evidence points to the conclusion that Yahwe was worshiped originally by

[164] In the third of this series of papers, treating of the historical significance of the Kenite Document, to appear in a subsequent volume of this *Annual*.

[165] Cf. the presence of Heber the Kenite in the north at the time of the Battle of Taanach, and the rôle played by his wife, Yael, therein, Jud. 4. 11 ff.; 5. 6, 24 ff.

[166] According to Jud. 18. 30 it was the grandson of Moses who became first the family or clan priest of Micah, and then the tribal priest of Dan. In other words, already the third generation of Levites in Palestine had begun to play the rôle of priests of Yahwe among the different tribes.

northern tribes independently of the late influence of the southern tribes, and especially of the Levites; therefore, instead of there having been one original Yahwe, as is generally assumed by scholars, Yahwe was probably a generic or class name for a group of early, desert, pastoral deities, worshiped by the various desert clans or tribes, the forerunners of the later tribes of Israel. In other words, there were originally, in all probability, numerous Yahwes, associated with different desert localities, and worshiped by different clans or tribes.[167] The worship of these various local, desert, tribal Yahwes was carried to Palestine by the migrating clans or tribes, was considerably modified there by contact with superior Canaanite civilization and Ba'al worship, and gradually coalesced into the conception of an intertribal, and eventually of a national Yahwe.

Accordingly, while positive, final evidence is lacking, and the possibility of a different process of evolution must be admitted, as has been said, the weight of evidence points to the conclusion that the original deity of the ark was a Yahwe, the Yahwe of Ephraim, or whatever the clan forerunners of Ephraim may have been.

And whatever the contents of the ark may have been, a sacred stone in all likelihood, or something else, it probably came from that spot in the desert where this Yahwe had been thought to dwell originally. In this particular object this Yahwe was from the very first believed to reside. Probably in it he had been worshiped by the ancestors of Ephraim; and when they migrated from their original desert home and sought a new and permanent abode in Palestine, they carried the sacred

---

[167] This hypothesis would also account adequately for the manifest regard for Yahwe as a deity in northern Syria, as evidenced by the names of the king of Hamath, Ilubi'di = Jaubi'di, and the name of the king of Ja'udi, Azrijau. (Cf. Meyer, *Die Israeliten und ihre Nachbarstämme*, 247 f.) The appearance of these names, in which Yahwe is manifestly an element, may be due either to direct Israelite influence, since the monuments upon which they are inscribed date from the 8th century B.C., or they may be due to the settlement in northern Syria at an early date of Aramaean tribes, probably akin to Israel, who had likewise worshiped Yahwe, or a Yahwe, out in the desert, and had carried his worship with them into their new home, precisely as Israel did.

object with them in the ark. Not improbably already out in the desert they had carried this object about with them in the ark upon their seasonal migrations from one encampment and one place of pasturage to another, and had believed that it guided them upon these journeyings and brought them surely and safely to the place where they could find abundance of water and pasturage for their flocks. In all likelihood too they carried this sacred object in the ark with them into battle against their desert foes, and confidently believed that it ensured them victory and abundant booty. Probably to it and its irresistible power they attributed their triumph over their Canaanite predecessors in the land, and particularly such significant achievements as the capture of the fortified city of Bethel.[168] Not impossibly even at the Battle of Taanach it was carried into battle by its tribesmen, and to its presence there the victory of the tribes of Israel over their powerful and feared Canaanite foes may have been attributed. In such case we can the more readily account for the leading rôle which Ephraim played among the northern tribes during the greater part of the remainder of the tribal period and for the developing rôle of intertribal deity which the Yahwe of the ark of Ephraim seemingly came to play during this period.

[168] Jud. 1. 22–26. In v. 22 the statement that when the Joseph-tribes went up to besiege Bethel Yahwe was with them, raises a question of interest and significance for this study. The statement here is not couched in the same manner as its parallel in v. 19, nor has it here apparently the same general significance as there. There it accounts for the unfailing success of Judah's efforts to conquer the southern portion of Palestine by the explanation that Yahwe was with them, i.e. that He prospered their various undertakings. In v. 22, however, the statement יהוה עמם seems to be somewhat more specific. The question suggests itself therefore, does this refer to the ark? When the Joseph-tribes went up against Bethel, did they take the ark with them, and did they accordingly attribute their capture of this fortified city to the presence of Yahwe, represented by the ark, in their midst? Knowing the rôle which the ark played in the Ephraimite practice of warfare, just this would have been the expected procedure. And in such case this passage would indicate that the ark and its contents were brought by the Joseph-tribes with them into Canaan, and were therefore of desert, and not of Canaanite origin. This is, however, merely a suggestion; for it must be admitted that the exact implication of the words יהוה עמם is too vague and uncertain to permit resting any absolute conclusion upon them.

And one additional bit of evidence tends to corroborate this general conclusion, furnished by Num. 10. 35 f. It requires but a moment's thought to realize that these two verses have only an incidental and not at all original connection with v. 33 b.[169] That verse speaks of the ark as the divine guide of Israel though the desert. These verses conceive of the ark as going into battle with the hosts of Israel and giving them victory over their enemy. It is true that, as we have seen, both of these tasks were regular functions of the ark during the first period of its history. But in this particular connection there is not the slightest reason for mentioning the latter function. Unquestionably vv. 35 f. are not a part of the original Book of the Covenant, but were appended later, although undoubtedly still at a fairly early date, by some writer or editor who was familiar with them and knew perfectly well of their bearing upon the ark. This is borne out by the connection with v. 33 b provided by this editor in v. 35 a, seeking to make the words of vv. 35 b and 36 apply to the setting forth of the ark upon each successive day's journey upon this march through the desert to the final goal of Israel's migration, rather than to its going forth to and return from battle, as the actual content of the two verses implies. Manifestly the thought of v. 35 a has no connection at all with that of vv. 35 b–36, and serves only to link these two verses with v. 33 b, with which also they have no immediate nor original connection.

But vv. 35 b–36 are in themselves unquestionably of considerable antiquity, in all likelihood older than the actual composition of the Book of the Covenant. It is of little moment for this study whether for the שׁוּבָה of v. 35 we

---

[169] V. 34, is, of course, P, and a very late insertion. In this connection it is interesting to note that the Rabbis of old likewise had a strong feeling that Num. 10. 35–36 were not in their proper and logical place; consequently, with their customary dialectic methods, they tried to justify their location here. But R. Ashi, probably more venturesome than the majority of his colleagues, dared to suggest that these verses had stood originally in connection with Num. 1. 52 and 2. 1 ff. and 34, and that the entire passage should have come at the end of Num. 2, but had been broken up and transposed in some unknown manner.

should read שֻׁבָה, with practically all modern scholars, and how we should interpret or emend the extremely difficult יהוה רבבות אלפי ישראל.[170] The fact is clear that here too the deity of the ark goes by the name Yahwe, and that he is here more than the mere tribal deity of Ephraim, is instead an intertribal deity, the deity of Israel.[171] These two verses, so plainly couched in poetic form, were undoubtedly the battle-cries of these tribes of Israel when going into battle with the ark of Yahwe in their midst, and when returning from battle after the victory had been gained.[172] The first

[170] For an interesting and ingenious, although I can not but feel, a rather far-fetched and untenable interpretation of this passage, cf. Torczyner, *op. cit.*, 223 ff.

[171] Israel here probably means primarily the closely related group of central tribes, the so-called Joseph-tribes, Ephraim, Manasseh and Benjamin, who apparently entered Palestine together under the leadership of Joshua, probably about 1350–1300 B.C., coming from the east and crossing the Jordan near Jericho. Whatever the origin of the name Israel may have been, it was probably applied originally to this particular group of clans or tribes, and may even have been borne by them out in the desert, before their entrance into Palestine. From them, due largely to the domination of these tribes, and especially Ephraim, from the time of the Battle of Taanach on, the name probably expanded to cover the entire group of northern tribes, bound together into a loose kind of federation growing out of the common victory gained over a common enemy at this important battle. It was probably to the original nucleus of the Joseph tribes, dwelling in central Palestine, that the name Israel upon the Merneptah inscription (circ. 1230 B.C.) referred (cf. Meyer, *Die Israeliten und ihre Nachbarstämme,* 222 ff.).

[172] For battle-cries of the modern Bedouin cf. Musil, *Arabia Petraea,* III, 386 ff. These show some slight similarity to Num. 10. 35 b–36; cf. in particular the battle-cry of the Tijâha, *edbaḥo, lâ jemlos,* "Kill him, so that he will not escape!"; However, but few, if any, of these Bedouin battle-cries are addressed to a deity, as are Num. 10. 35 b–36. Many of them are semi-meaningless, while some are addressed to the enemy and others are calls to fellow-warriors. Such battle-cries are those of the Terâbîn, *ṣubjân jâ terâbîn, birâke' el-ḥejl,* "Be heroes, O Terabin, in the stabbing of the horses!"; of the Rawarne of eṣ-Ṣâfije, *ṣubjân jâ zoṛârne,* "Be heroes, O Zorarne!," and of the 'Amârîn, *ṣubjân jâ nišâma, ṣubjân jâ ḥâbbin ar-rîḥ; hejlâ 'alejku biẓ-ẓafar, ṣubjân jâ bawârdijje,* "Be brave, O heroes, be brave, you who are swifter than the wind; forward, on to victory, be brave O you warriors!" These last are strikingly similar to the cry of the Philistines before going into the Battle of Eben Haezer, התחזקו והיו לאנשים פלשתים, "Be strong, and show yourselves men, O Philistines!" (I Sam. 4. 9 a. The remainder of the verse, and the turn given by it to this battle-cry, are in all likelihood not original.)

cry was undoubtedly sounded by the Israelite warriors when going into the Battle of Eben Haezer; because of the unexpected outcome of this battle they had no opportunity to sound the second cry upon this occasion. But if the ark was present at the Battle of Taanach, as there is every reason to suppose, they had then, as well as no doubt upon numerous other occasions, opportunity to sound both cries. Certainly these two cries must have had some history behind them. They could not have come into existence just at the time of, nor even shortly before the capture of the ark by the Philistines. But this consideration points positively to the conclusion that for a considerable time back, perhaps as far back as the Battle of Taanach, or quite probably even earlier than this, the ark must have been the intertribal palladium and Yahwe the intertribal deity at least of that small group of clans or tribes which constituted the original federation known by the name of Israel, viz. the Joseph-tribes, Ephraim, Manasseh (Machir, Abi-Ezer, &c.) and Benjamin.

VII

SUMMARY OF THE HISTORY OF THE ARK

Summing up all this evidence we must conclude that the ark contained a sacred object in which Yahwe, the tribal deity of Ephraim, was thought to dwell. This object, most probably a sacred stone, had probably stood originally in the desert, perhaps upon a mountain out there. The presence of this deity in this object made this spot sacred, the place of gathering and of simple religious worship by some one clan or tribe, or perhaps some small group of clans or tribes. When this clan or tribe or tribal group migrated from their original desert home, and sought a new and permanent abode in the country west of the Jordan, they carried with them, in its ark, in which perhaps it had already been housed during the desert period, this sacred object with the deity residing in it. They looked upon it as their faithful and unerring guide through the desert, particularly through stretches with which they were but little familiar. They were accustomed also to carry it with them into battle, at least into decisive battles, and to attribute to its presence and assistance all victories gained in such battles. They likewise looked to it for oracular revelation and decision.

Settled permanently in Palestine the ark was eventually deposited in Shiloh in the territory of the tribe of Ephraim, in a suitable sanctuary, and in time a Levitical family came to function as its priests. Located here this ark served not only as the particular cult-object and palladium of Ephraim, but also at quite an early period it came to enjoy a large inter-tribal reputation and authority, at least among those seemingly related tribes which constituted the federation of Israel. And not improbably it enjoyed a considerable measure of authority and veneration also among those more remotely related tribes, who had apparently entered Palestine at an even earlier period than did these tribes of Israel, but whose fortunes came to be intimately bound up with those of Israel by the common danger threatening all from the original Canaanite inhabitants of the land, and especially by the outcome of the decisive battle of Taanach.

Captured by the Philistines in the Battle of Eben Haezer, the ark remained for a short time in their possession. But, concluding from a series of calamities which befell them during this period that the ark was, despite its capture by them, still a powerful and dangerous deity, they allowed it to depart from their possession and their land, after first submitting it to a decisive test to prove its divinity and its continued power. After an unfortunate experience at Beth Shemesh, the ark came to reside for a period of approximately a century at Kiryath Yearim. Why during this period its original worshipers apparently made no effort to reclaim it, particularly since it had proved its persistent divine nature and power both by its triumph over the Philistines and by the blessings which it undoubtedly brought upon the household of Abinadab, in which it was deposited, and upon all the people of Kiryath Yearim, just as later it brought through its presence similar blessings upon the household of Obed-Edom, it is difficult to imagine.

Seemingly the process would not have been difficult, since Kiryath Yearim lay apparently in the territory of Benjamin, and the Benjamites under Saul had taken up the battle against the Philistines, and were endeavoring to enhearten their northern neighbors and win their support in this war for freedom. It might be expected that the restoration to them of their old palladium would have revived the spirits of these northern tribes and made them valuable allies for Saul. But in all likelihood the people of Kiryath Yearim, experiencing the benefit of the presence of this sacred object in their midst, were unwilling to part with it. And not impossibly too the northern tribes had during this eventful century advanced a bit culturally and outgrown somewhat their former conception of and reverence for the ark. And quite probably too their deep-rooted fear of the Philistines deterred them from bringing back the ark into their midst; for such an act would, of course, have been tantamount to a declaration of rebellion against the Philistines; and this they did not dare.

At any rate the ark remained in Kiryath Yearim until brought up to Jerusalem by David. The probable reasons for this have already been discussed. It was undoubtedly removed by Solomon from David's tent-sanctuary to his more magnificent Temple. That is the last definite information about the ark that the Bible furnishes. Thereafter the ark is an object only of unhistoric tradition and legend, with little foundation on actual fact. This serves to show clearly the development of theological thought in Israel, but in no wise furnishes authentic historic information about the ark itself.

Undoubtedly the ark continued in the Temple down to the destruction by Nebuchadrezzar in 586 B.C., or perhaps only until the first deportation and plundering of the Temple in 597 B.C. During this period, under the influence of developing national Yahwe religion and of advance in theological thought and concept of Yahwe, due to the teachings of the prophets, the ark came to be looked upon more or less askance as, according to old and not completely forgotten tradition, a concrete representation of Yahwe; therefore, in accordance with the principles of the evolving theology, as an idolatrous, non-Yahwistic object, altogether out of accord with the true, prophetic concept and worship of Him. But it escaped the fate of destruction which would undoubtedly have eventually overtaken it, just as it overtook the brazen serpent, apparently an object of kindred character, and in all likelihood of kindred origin, by undergoing a process of reinterpretation and legitimization. It came gradually to be regarded as the receptacle of a sacred stone, or rather of two sacred stones; but sacred now, not because a deity was thought to reside in them, but only incidentally, because Israel's national Yahwe had inscribed upon them the ten "words" which constituted the fundamental principles of His worship and the basis of His covenant with Israel. Looked upon in this light, the ark was suffered to remain in the Temple at Jerusalem. But apparently its original character was never entirely lost sight of by the prophetic party; and particularly during the last century or so of its sojourn in the Temple it seems to have experienced a gradual diminution in esteem. During the early portion of the post-exilic period, even after the second Temple had been erected, the absence of the ark therefrom was not even deplored, at least by the prophetic party.

But with the ascendency of the Priestly party in the period following Ezra, and with the composition of the Grundschrift and secondary portions of the Priestly Code, the ark came to enjoy a new regard and greatly increased in significance. It became intimately associated in Priestly tradition with the *kebod Yahwe*, the fiery form, ordinarily enveloped in the cloud, which Yahwe was thought to assume in His immediate contacts with Israel. In addition to maintaining the older tradition of the ark as the receptacle of the two tablets of the Decalogue, now known as the "tablets of testimony," these Priestly theologians and writers now represented it also and primarily as the throne of Yahwe, upon which He was believed to dwell permanently but invisibly, in the holy of holies, in the midst of Israel. Only the high-priest, and he only once a year, and then only under the precaution of all manner of safe-guards and the observance of innumerable taboos, was permitted to enter into Yahwe's presence before the ark in the holy of holies, and catch a fleeting glimpse of the Holy One upon His sacred throne, the ark. Tradition is silent as to the eventual fate of the ark when the Temple was finally destroyed by the Romans.[173] Actually, however, both historic evidence and Rabbinic tradition seem to agree that there never was an ark in the second Temple, and that the picture of the Priestly Code is naught but the product of extensive theological speculation coupled with an antiquarian interest in the religious institutions of Israel's past and a desire to reinterpret these to accord with the dominant theology of the late post-exilic period and so give them a legitimate place in Israel's religion.

Such seems to have been the full history of the ark in ancient Israel.

VIII

THE ARK IN THE BOOK OF THE COVENANT

In the light of this history of the ark, as we have reconstructed it, the question naturally arises, why is the ark mentioned at all in the Book of the Covenant; what rôle does it play there, and what purpose does the mention of it serve? The question is difficult to answer with any certainty, since the reference to the ark in C is brief and obscure; yet it is a question of obvious importance, that must at least be considered as fully as possible.

On the basis of carefully considered internal evidence we have reached the conclusion that the nucleus of the Book of the Covenant, i. e. the small narrative setting plus the "words," was composed in the Northern Kingdom in 842 B.C., and constituted the basis of the religious reformation of Elisha, supported by Jehu and the Rechabites, under their leader Jonadab ben Rechab. This conclusion was reached as the result of first fixing the date of the Kenite Document as 899 B.C., its place of composition as the Southern Kingdom, and its purpose to enforce

---

[173] According to apocryphal and rabbinical tradition the ark was one of the five sacred objects hidden away by God when the Temple was destroyed and destined to be restored when the Messiah should come and rebuild the Temple. (II Mac. 2. 4-6; Bammidbar rabba, XV, 7; *Jewish Encyclopedia*, II, 105 f.)

the far-reaching religious reformation which in his fifteenth year King Asa, influenced by the prophetic party, which in turn had unmistakably a Kenite or Rechabite background, succeeded in carrying out. This reformation was directed chiefly against the foreign religious and cultural influences which had crept into the life and religious practice of the people, and even into the cult of the Temple at Jerusalem, from the days of David and Solomon onward. It aimed to restore what its champions conceived to have been the true, simple worship of Yahwe, as it had been practiced by the ancestors of the southern tribes, and particularly as it had been, so they thought, revealed by Yahwe to Moses after the exodus from Egypt, and by Moses in turn communicated to Israel. According to their tradition, upon this occasion a covenant had been established between Yahwe and these Israelite tribes, through the mediation of Moses, whereby Israel obligated itself to worship Yahwe alone and in accordance with the fundamental principles of His worship, revealed by Yahwe to Moses in a set of "words," and Yahwe on His part, obligated Himself to bring these tribes to and settle them in a good land, and be with them and prosper them ever thereafter. According to the historical record, this traditional covenant between Yahwe and Israel, made in the desert, was reaffirmed and properly solemnized at Jerusalem in the year 899 B.C., when the people gathered there for the celebration of the festival in the third month, the festival later known as Shabuoth.

Now, as we have seen, the relationship of the "words" of the Book of the Covenant to those of the Kenite Document is so obvious and so close that the conclusion can not be escaped that the former are dependent upon the latter. As the result of a minute comparison of the "words" of K with those of C, and a determination of the relative cultural background of the two sets of "words," we have likewise concluded that the "words" of C, and with them, of course, the original Book of the Covenant, must have been composed in the Northern Kingdom, and, it follows, at a time somewhat later than the date of composition of K. It is clear, moreover, from the determination of the cultural background of C, that it must have been composed at a time when the Northern Kingdom had experienced a period of economic prosperity and cultural progress, when images of gold and silver were by no means unknown, nor even uncommon, in the ritual practice of the people, and elaborate altars of hewn stones were likewise employed. Such a condition obtained only during the reigns of Ahab and his immediate successors, when Israel not only succeeded in winning for itself a sure and recognized place among the leading states of western Asia, but likewise enjoyed an extended term of comparative peace and quiet, which enabled its citizens to follow their economic pursuits with comparatively little disturbance and interruption, and to experience the resultant material prosperity.

This national prosperity was strengthened and stimulated by Ahab's marriage with Jezebel, the Phoenician princess. This was in strict accord with the established political principles of the time, and in full conformity with the policy which Solomon had followed earlier and seemingly upon a more extensive scale. Jezebel, an ardent devotee of her own ancestral and national deity, brought with her to Israel and to Ahab's court the worship of the Baal of Tyre and also a numerous retinue of personal attendants and religious ministrants. Phoenician influence now began to modify the cultural life of Israel more and more, and the worship of the Baal of Tyre to make steady and rapid headway. Images of this Baal were set up, presumably in various parts of the country, and certainly in the sanctuaries at Samaria and Jezreel. And if the traditions of the Books of Kings are to be accepted, not content with this, Jezebel attempted to make active and aggressive propaganda for the spread of the worship of the Baal of Tyre throughout Israel. In this she encountered the strong opposition of the prophetic party under the leadership, tacit at least, of first Elijah and, after his death, Elisha.

Elijah, a shepherd from east of the Jordan and a firm, uncompromising champion of the old, simple, nomadic or semi-nomadic worship of Yahwe, conceived of Yahwe, as we have seen,[174] as still dwelling out in the desert upon the mountain

---

[174] " The Oldest Document, &c.," *HUCA*, IV (1927), 32 ff.

where, according to the Kenite tradition, Israel first came in contact and entered into covenant with Him after the exodus from Egypt.[175] He opposed the plans of Jezebel unremittingly during his lifetime, but on the whole seemingly with comparatively little practical success. His method was that of bitter, fearless, uncompromising denunciation of the powerful queen and her god. He acted independently and had but little immediate contact and direct cooperation with the professional prophets of his day, for his methods, as well as his prophetic call, were largely different than theirs. But his authority and superior rating as a prophet, called directly and personally by Yahwe, were apparently fully recognized by them. After his death his disciple Elisha seemingly continued his master's methods for a time. Eventually, however, no doubt becoming convinced that no real and practical results were to be achieved by these methods and that the worship of Baal in Israel could never be uprooted in this way, Elisha resorted to different methods, the methods employed by the

[175] It is indeed a strange and significant fact that Elijah, apparently a native of Gilead, should conceive of Yahwe and His dwelling-place in quite the same manner as did the Kenites, dwelling in the extreme southern part of Judah. The suggestion has been advanced by some scholar, whose name and likewise the reference to whose work have escaped me, that Elijah may not have been a native of Gilead, but only a stranger and sojourner there. He bases his argument chiefly upon the statement of I Ki. 17. 1 that Elijah was one of the "sojourners of Gilead" (מתשבי גלעד), and argues that this points to a non-Gileadite origin for Elijah. In such case, of course, it would be natural to regard Elijah's original home as in the extreme south, in the vicinity of the Kenites. This would account completely for Elijah's ardent championing of Yahwe, and for his believing, along with the Kenites and the prophetic party of the south, that Yahwe still dwelt upon "the mountain of Yahwe" in the desert. If the reading מִתֹּשָׁבֵי גִלְעָד of I Ki. 17. 1 is original and correct, then this hypothesis is extremely plausible. But it is by no means unlikely that it is a dittography and misreading of an original הַתִּשְׁבִּי (cf. the *Commentaries* of Kittel and Benzinger to the passage). In such case, of course, Elijah must be regarded as a native Gileadite. Then the question as to how Elijah came to hold this view of Yahwe in common with the Kenites would remain unanswered for lack of evidence. His native shepherd life and point of view would account for his conceiving of Yahwe in the old, traditional, semi-nomadic manner, but it would hardly account for his holding to the Kenite-Judahite belief that Yahwe still dwelt upon this particular mountain in the desert.

professional prophets in the Northern Kingdom upon two previous occasions, when the dynasties of Jerobeam I and Baasha were overthrown. Elisha made common cause with the professional prophets and employed one of them as his agent in anointing Jehu as king of Israel. In the revolution which followed the entire house of Ahab was murdered. Jehu became ruler of the Northern Kingdom. And, supported by Jonadab ben Rechab, he gathered under a pretext all the devotees of the Tyrian Baal, undoubtedly members of the court party, the followers of Jezebel, into the sanctuary at Samaria, and there butchered them in cold blood.[176] This act had the unqualified approval, and probably even the cooperation, of Jonadab ben Rechab and no doubt of Elisha also. In this way the worship of the Baal of Tyre was uprooted from Israelite life and practice, and, at least on the surface, the old worship of Yahwe was restored.

Externally this reformation bears a strong resemblance to that of Asa in 899 B.C., fifty-seven years earlier. In both cases a woman, the queen, and then, after her husband's death, the queen-mother, is the leader of the court party, and the chief champion of the worship of foreign, non-Yahwistic deities, and foreign cultural influence. In both cases the opposition is fostered by the prophetic party, unmistakably in contact with and under direct Kenite or Rechabite influence. And in both cases the reformation directs itself externally and concretely to the destruction of images regarded as non-Yahwistic and symbolic of foreign deities.[177] In particular the

[176] II Ki. 10. 15–29.

[177] It is not at all improbable that the reformation of Elisha-Jehu-Jonadab ben Rechab was likewise sealed with a covenant ceremony, similar to that by which the reformation of Asa was sealed, according to II Chron. 15. 12 ff. It is true that II Ki. 10. 15–29 makes no mention of such a covenant; but it is difficult to avoid the impression that the narrative here is incomplete. Certainly the reformation itself, to be thoroughly effective, required not merely the butchery of the worshipers of the Tyrian Baal, but also the formal rejection of the worship of this deity and a declaration of loyalty to Yahwe by Israel; and this would, of course, imply a renewal or reaffirmation of the covenant between Yahwe and Israel. In all likelihood therefore, some such record stood in the original account of this important event. We can well understand, furthermore, why this record should have been suppressed and omitted from

Kenite influence manifest in K and the participation of Jonadab ben Rechab, member of a Kenite clan, in the reformation of Elisha, suggest a direct relationship between the reformation in the Southern Kingdom in 899 B.C. and this reformation in the Northern Kingdom fifty-seven years later. And this suggestion is strongly confirmed by the close and direct dependence of the " words " of the Book of the Covenant upon those of K, which we have established. This evidence suffices to establish with utmost probability that the original Book of the Covenant constituted the basis of the reformation of Elisha-Jehu-Jonadab ben Rechab in 842 B.C., just as the Kenite code of "words" constituted the basis of the reformation of Asa in 899 B.C. It follows therefore with reasonable certainty that the date of composition of the "words" of the Book of the Covenant, together with their narrative setting, must have been 842 B.C.

But then our question, how account for the mention of the ark in the Book of the Covenant? And this question becomes all the more pertinent and striking when we realize that at just this time, in 842 B.C., the ark was no longer in the possession of the northern tribes, nor present anywhere in the Northern Kingdom, but was deposited in the Temple at Jerusalem, and had in fact been there uninterruptedly ever

this passage in II Ki. 10, and why all reference to this event is omitted entirely from Chron. It was, of course, because the later prophets and their followers, the prophetic party of a later day, disapproved most heartily of this wholesale murder of the worshipers of Baal by Jehu and denounced it as a crime incurring the wrath of Yahwe (cf. Hos. 1. 4; 2. 2). With such a prophetic judgment upon this act, later prophetic and priestly writers could not well record, nor even acknowledge, that the event was crowned by the solemnization of a covenant between Yahwe and Israel; hence their complete silence about this covenant ceremony. But if we admit that in all probability this reformation of Elisha-Jehu-Jonadab ben Rechab, with all its hideous details of betrayal, murder and butchery, was climaxed by a solemnization of the covenant between Yahwe and Israel, its parallelism with the reformation of Asa becomes complete in all essential features. And not only this, but its relation to the Book of the Covenant, with its record of the original solemnization of the covenant between Yahwe and Israel in the days of Moses, recorded in Ex. 24. 4–8, of which this last solemnization in 842 B.C. was, so it would naturally be interpreted, merely the renewal or reaffirmation, would become doubly clear.

since the erection of this Temple a century or more before this. And not merely that, but the ark had been gone from the possession of and presence among the northern tribes for approximately two hundred and fifty years, and the knowledge and memory of it must have become extremely weak by 842 B.C. Its mention therefore in this northern document, and the reference to the early function as divine guide through the desert which, as we have seen, ancient tradition ascribed to it, are surprising indeed. There must have been some reason for such reference.

In answer to this question only a conjecture can be offered, due, of course, to total lack of evidence; but a conjecture so natural and fitting as to render it extremely plausible and illuminating. The reformation of 842 B.C. was directed primarily against the worship of the Tyrian Baal in Israel and the image-cult and foreign cultural influence associated with it. It sought to reaffirm and reestablish the old worship of Yahwe as the true, national god of Israel. The concept of Yahwe underlying this reformation was that which had been held and cherished out in the desert in the early, semi-nomadic days, the concept which had been zealously guarded and boldly championed by the Kenites and Rechabites and by Elijah, the shepherd prophet. It was a concept which had been touched and modified, particularly in the agricultural Northern Kingdom, by contact with Canaanitish Baals and the resultant syncretism; yet in it semi-nomadic, desert features still predominated; and it was upon these that the prophetic program laid the main emphasis. Stated generally and as a basic principle, this reformation aimed to root out foreign, Baal-worship from Israel, and to restore the old, native Yahwe-worship, rooted in semi-nomadic life and desert ideas and ideals.

But how symbolize this old, native, desert Yahwe? We have seen [178] that in the reformation of 899 B.C. in the Southern Kingdom Yahwe and His true worship were symbolized by the old "tent of meeting," while the syncretistic worship, with its manifold foreign elements, against which

---

[178] "The Oldest Document, &c.," *HUCA*, IV (1927), 119-127.

this reformation contended, was apparently symbolized by the *mifleṣet* of Maachah, the queen-mother, and probably also by similar images associated with this syncretistic worship, and perhaps even by the recently erected Temple at Jerusalem in which this worship was centralized. In the reformation of 842 B.C. in the Northern Kingdom the symbol of the false, syncretistic worship, against which the reformation was directed, must have been, of course, the image or images of the Tyrian Baal which Jezebel had set up in the various sanctuaries. What fitting symbol of the old, native, desert Yahwe could there be, which would represent Him fittingly in the eyes of the people of the Northern Kingdom? Certainly it could not be the "tent of meeting," for, on the one hand, as we have seen, this had been the cult-object only of the southern tribes, and differed radically in its original character from the various cult-objects of the northern tribes. And on the other hand, in the one respect of reintroducing the old "tent of meeting," in opposition to the Temple at Jerusalem, the reformation of 899 B.C. had failed; and with this failure the old "tent of meeting" must have forfeited much of its pristine regard and have passed practically into semi-oblivion. Certainly it was no proper and effective symbol of the old Yahwe for the northern tribes.

But what symbol more natural and fitting could there be than the ark? It had been the palladium of the northern tribes during the days of their greatest triumphs in the early period of settlement in Palestine. It had been the cult-object of Ephraim, and eventually too of the other tribes federated with Ephraim. According to firmly rooted tradition, it had led them upon their desert journeyings until they were permanently settled in Palestine, and had gone with them into battle and given them victory over their enemies; it had established them securely in the land and prospered them in all their early undertakings. It was of desert origin and associated with the name and worship of Yahwe from those ancient days. Therefore, contrasted with the Tyrian Baal and his images, it was for the people of the Northern Kingdom the true symbol of Yahwe. And a moment's thought shows clearly that no other object whatsoever could have played this important rôle in this northern reformation, for no other ancient cult-object had enjoyed the same regard and authority among the northern tribes in the early tribal days.[179]

Moreover, the very condition that the ark was no longer in the possession of the northern tribes, but was located in the Temple at Jerusalem, facilitated this process. For, on the one hand, as the result of the absence of the ark from their midst, and the fact that it had been gone for two hundred and fifty years, these northern tribes could have had only a more or less vague, traditional, but no real knowledge of the ark and its actual appearance and its full, original nature and function. Their conception of Yahwe as their national deity had certainly advanced materially during this momentous period, and they could no longer conceive of Him in quite the same primitive manner as did their tribal ancestors. To them there was probably hardly any question of Yahwe, no longer merely a tribal, but now a national deity, actually being in the ark, or of there being in it a sacred stone or some other similar object in which Yahwe was thought to dwell. By this time this belief must have been largely, if not entirely outgrown, and in the minds of the northern tribes, so far as they thought of the ark at all, which was probably very little, it must have come gradually to be regarded as the symbol of Yahwe rather than as Yahwe Himself, or as the container of Yahwe. And on the other hand, the very presence of the ark in the Temple at Jerusalem must have given to it, even in the eyes of the people of the Northern Kingdom, a new sanctity and legitimacy as a symbol of Yahwe, their national god, which it would otherwise not have enjoyed. Even to the leaders of this prophetic movement this fact must have had a deep significance. Had the ark been still merely

---

[179] Thus, for example, the cult-object of the tribe of Dan was of Palestinian origin (Jud. 17–18), and apparently also the cult-object of Manasseh (Jud. 8. 24–27). Not improbably this was true also of the cult-objects of some of the other northern tribes. In fact the ark is the only ancient, northern, tribal cult-object of which we have any record, which goes back to a pre-Palestinian, desert origin and association with the worship of Yahwe there.

what it had been in the early, pre-Davidic days, they could
hardly have sanctioned it, and referred to it in their program
of reformation; for it would unquestionably have seemed to
them too concrete a representation of Yahwe, differing but
little, if at all, from the representation of Him by images,
against which they protested so steadily. But the presence
of the ark in the Temple at Jerusalem must have completed
the process of gradual reinterpretation of it, from its original
character as a Yahwe-cult-object to its new character as a
Yahwe-symbol, and must have likewise given it, even for
these prophetic champions, a certain positive legitimacy and
sanctity, which it could otherwise not have acquired.

And so very naturally they revived the memory of the
old ark of Yahwe among the northern tribesmen and represented it as the approved symbol of Yahwe, the true, national
god of Israel and god of Israel's fathers. Thereby they
declared concretely to the citizens of the Northern Kingdom
of their own day that this old Yahwe, whose origin was in
the desert, was still their true god, and not the new, foreign
deity whom Jezebel and her court party had sought to foist
upon them. It was Yahwe who had prospered them through
all these years and given them victory over their enemies and
a proud and leading place among the states of Western Asia.
And to Him alone their faith and their worship were due,
even as they had covenanted with Him in the ancient, desert
days. And this true god of theirs, Yahwe, was to be worshiped
in accordance with the simple principles and by the simple
rites, theoretically at least, and to a large extent factually
also, of desert origin, set forth now in the "words" of the
Book of the Covenant. This was their true worship and not
the more elaborate worship of Baal in Baal sanctuaries, with
their altars of hewn stones, probably with steps leading upon
them, with images of gold and silver, with abundant and
extensive sacrifices and festivals of a dominantly agricultural,
solar character. The program of the reformation of 842 B.C.
was decidedly reactionary, just as that of the reformation of
899 B.C. had been. It sought to reintroduce the simple altar
of earth in place of the altars of hewn stone, just as the

reformation of 899 B.C. had in all likelihood attempted to reintroduce the old "tent of meeting" in place of the new, elaborate Temple at Jerusalem. And just as that reformation had failed in this one reactionary purpose, so in all likelihood this reformation of 842 B.C. also failed in its effort to reintroduce the simple, earthen altar.[180] The course of cultural progress can not be lightly turned backward.

In this program of reformation the ark had its definite place and served a specific and valuable purpose. But it could not be as the old ark unmodified from its original, primitive character and functions. The presence of the ark in the Temple at Jerusalem required a fitting explanation that would legitimize it and give it a definite place in the program of this reformation. The old traditions of the sanctity and powers of the ark, no doubt rather vague and shadowy by this time, and not altogether free from illegitimate, idolatrous implications, had to be put aside altogether, and a new interpretation of it presented, which would, on the one hand, accord fully with the conception of Yahwe held by these reformers, and, on the other hand, would further their cherished program as much as possible. Unquestionably it was under the force of these conditions that the new tradition developed that the ark was sacred, yes, and sacred because of what it contained; this much survived from the old tradition. But what it contained, so it now came to be told, was merely the record of the covenant between Yahwe and Israel, the scroll of the "words" of the covenant, which Moses had written down at Yahwe's bidding in the old, desert days. Thus, on the one hand, the ark came to have a traditional association with Moses, something which it could hardly have had previous to this,[181] and, on the other hand, it now became even more than the symbol of Yahwe Himself; it became the symbol and the constant

[180] Therefore no doubt the secondary, but certainly still quite early, provision of Ex. 20. 25, that if Israel insists upon building stone altars, they must at least not be of hewn stones.

[181] Unless perhaps through its Levitical priests, Eli and his sons, probably in some way akin to Moses. The name Pinchas, borne by Eli's son and also by Moses' great-nephew, the grandson of Aaron, according to Priestly tradition, and itself of Egyptian origin, may well support such a conclusion.

reminder to the people of His covenant with Israel; from this time on it was the ארון ברית יהוה, "the ark of the covenant of Yahwe." Such must have been its official name henceforth. And this very name and its frequent repetition must have had a potent effect in redeeming the ark from all its earlier, traditional, idolatrous implications as a tribal cult-object and concrete representation of Yahwe, and giving it a definite, legitimate place in prophetic tradition and program and in the subsequent evolution of the religion of Israel.

In this way and at this time, in all likelihood, the new, prophetic tradition about the ark and its sacred character arose and supplanted the older and historically more correct tradition. And later, and no doubt still somewhat under the influence of the old tradition of the probable presence of a sacred stone in the ark, the new tradition was further modified slightly, to tell that, not a scroll, containing the "words" of the covenant, was in the ark, but two sacred stones, sacred, however, not because of an inherent sanctity or indwelling of any deity in them, but because the "words" of the covenant were inscribed upon them, and, moreover, inscribed upon them by Yahwe Himself. And, as we have seen, according to the northern Elohist version of this tradition, not only the writing, but even the stones themselves, prepared for writing, were the actual work of Yahwe; their sanctity was therefore absolute. So the new tradition about the ark and its contents developed. Its subsequent history we have already learned. There can be little further question as to the place of the ark in the tradition of the Book of the Covenant and the rôle which it played in the reformation of 842 B.C., of which the Book of the Covenant furnished the program.

Unquestionably the narrative setting of the Book of the Covenant must have once been more extensive than we know it at present. In particular it must have told more about the ark and the depositing in it of the scroll of the "words" by Moses. All this, however, has, for one reason or another, been suppressed by later editors, and only the small fragment of the original narrative setting contained in Ex. 24. 4–8 and

Num. 10. 33 b, and in all likelihood a small nucleus in Ex. 33. 5 b–6, have been preserved.[182] Of this no more can be said at

[182] It would be natural to expect that the narrative portion of the Book of the Covenant would have told something about the carriers of the ark. We have seen above (p. 20) that this must have told or implied that on the desert journey the ark was carried along on the shoulders of men, whom it drove irresistibly in the direction in which it chose to go. Presumably these bearers of the ark were not ordinary persons; they must have been men who stood in some particularly intimate relation to the deity of the ark. Who could they have been?

In answer to this question Deut. 10. 8 gives a significant hint. It tells that "at that time," i.e. at the time when Moses made the ark at Yahwe's command, and deposited the two tablets of the Decalogue in it (With בעת ההוא in v. 10 cf. the same expression in v. 1. Note also that vv. 6 and 7 are a Priestly gloss inserted into this context, and disturb the obviously original continuity between vv. 1–5 and v. 8.) Yahwe singled out the tribe of Levi to carry the ark. In v. 11 the Deuteronomic version of Yahwe's command to Israel to set out upon its journey through the wildernes is found, following immediately upon the account of the making of the ark and of the appointment of the Levites to carry it. The implication is clear that the Levites were the bearers of the ark upon the journey through the wilderness.

Obviously therefore the Deuteronomic authors of Deut. 10. 1–5, 8–11 must have had before them a narrative which told of these three incidents in connected form. We have had reason to conclude that the original of the narrative of the making of the ark in vv. 1–5, is to be found in Ex. 33. 5b–6, and that these verses stood originally in close juxtaposition to Ex. 34. 1–5 (above pp. 29 ff.). But we find no narrative of the selection of the Levites following this passage. However, in Ex. 32. 26–29, i.e. a passage almost immediately preceding Ex. 33. 5b–6, we find an account of the selection by Yahwe of the Levites, in order to bestow a blessing upon them. This passage is embedded in the narrative of the Golden Calf, but it is recognized by all scholars as a very disturbing element in this narrative, having little apparent connection with and explanation from the Golden Calf story. Unquestionably it is not in its original position in the Biblical narrative.

The passage is extremely difficult of explanation, due to its manifestly fragmentary character. It seems to imply that in Moses' absence the people of Israel had sinned grievously against Yahwe, and that only the Levites had remained faithful to Him. It does not state here wherein the sin of Israel had lain, nor likewise in what respect the Levites had remained faithful. But from Deut. 33. 9 it may be safely inferred that the sin of Israel was faithlessness to its covenant with Yahwe, whereas the Levites alone had kept the covenant. Therefore, Deut. 33. 10 goes on to say, the Levites have the high privilege of functioning as Yahwe's priests. Ex. 32. 26–29 unquestionably carries the same implication, that Israel's sin consisted in disregard of its covenant with Yahwe, but recently made. This motif fits perfectly into the C narrative, and makes it parallel the K narrative in one additional and significant detail.

present. It remains for us to consider now in detail the laws of the present Book of the Covenant, and particularly those laws which, seemingly, supplement the original "words." The "words" themselves we have already considered in sufficient detail, and little more can or need be added to what has been said.[183]

In the light of these considerations we may venture to infer that Ex. 32. 26–29 originally followed 33. 5b–6, and that the Deuteronomic authors of Deut. 10. 1–5, 8–11 found them there, still in their original position, and not yet dislocated to their present place in Ex. 32. In their original position they must have gone on to tell that the blessing which Yahwe bestowed upon these Levites as the reward for their faithfulness to Him and His covenant was the high privilege of carrying the ark, and of standing before Him, of ministering unto Him, and of uttering blessings in His name, as Deut. 10. 8 puts it, or of communicating His judgments and oracles to Israel and of bringing His chief sacrifices upon His altar, as Deut. 33. 10 has it. Just these functions were discharged by the Levitical priests of the ark of Yahwe at Shiloh, Eli and his household. Undoubtedly this is then the family tradition of the house of Eli, accounting for their selection by Yahwe to be His priests and the bearers of His ark, whether upon the journey through the wilderness or into battle with the Philistines or other enemies.

We may therefore conclude that Ex. 32. 26–29 was likewise originally a part of the Book of the Covenant and followed in the C narrative almost immediately after Ex. 33. 5b–6.

The meaning of the passage is, however, still obscure; nor does it seem possible to throw much further light upon it. It is not clear wherein the faithlessness of the people of Israel and their disregard for the newly-made covenant lay. Certainly it had nothing at all to do with the Golden Calf episode, for, as we have seen (" The Oldest Document of the Hexateuch," *HUCA*, IV [1927], 109 ff.), that narrative, in its original form, belonged entirely to the Kenite Document. Perhaps it may be inferred from Deut. 33. 8, that it had to do with a testing of the people in some way by Yahwe, at the place called therefore Massah, in order to prove their faithfulness; and only the Levites withstood the test. But wherein the test consisted and what was the consequent nature of Israel's faithlessness neither Ex. 32. 26–29 nor Deut. 33. 8 nor any of the later Biblical traditions about Massah and Meribah (Ex. 17. 1–7; Num. 20. 7–13) give the slightest hint. Manifestly it resulted in a violation in some way of the newly-made covenant, as the result of which Yahwe punished the offenders at the hands of the faithful Levites, and then commanded the people to leave His sacred mountain and set out upon their journey toward their מנוחה (Num. 10. 33), the land which Yahwe had promised to give them as a part of His l. covenant-obligation to them. On this journey through the wilderness they were led by the ark carried by the Levites. All this must have once constituted the concluding portion of the narrative of the Book of the Covenant.

[183] "The Oldest Document, &c.," *HUCA*, IV (1927), 54–98.

www.ingramcontent.com/pod-product-compliance
Lightning Source LLC
Chambersburg PA
CBHW071436160426
43195CB00013B/1929